Christians and Muslims at the Epicenter

Walter R. Ratliff

CONTENTS

WALTER R. RATLIFF

PREFACE

The cover of this book is an apt visual metaphor of what *Christians and Muslims at the Epicenter* is about. The photo was taken by a U.S. Marine sergeant on September 11, 2010. Twin shafts of blue light spring toward the heavens as a representation of the destroyed World Trade Center towers. A cloud intersects the lights, forming somewhat of a cross.

Among evangelicals, a person's relationship with God is often spoke of as "vertical." The strength of that vertical relationship has immense bearing on a Christian's "horizontal" relationships with other people. In the cover image, the vertical light appears brightest at two points – at its origin and where meets the cloud. A fissure emerges in this fleeting cross-shape as the cloud meets the light, just as evangelical responses to Muslims and the religion of Islam seems to have split in the decade after the Sept. 11th attacks. In many ways, evangelicals show a degree of unity when it comes to vertical issues, including the essentials of conservative theology, the reliability of the Bible, and the need to share the Gospel. However, the Sept. 11th attacks have caused a rift within the evangelical family over how to bring vertical principles to bear on new horizontal challenges.

September 11th marked a watershed moment within evangelical ideology. Evangelical responses to the challenges that came in the wake of the attacks varied within movement, betraying fault lines within evangelicalism that cut across denominational and regional lines. Following the attacks, Muslim advocacy groups reported a rise in hurtful rhetoric from the evangelical community coupled with an increase in the number of hate crimes against Muslims. Yet, as some evangelical leaders were portraying Islam as a violent religion and Muslims as a menace, other evangelicals were attempting to engage their American Muslim neighbors with dialogue and respect.

The attacks forced evangelicals to reconsider the challenge of Islam and its adherents in relation to the movement's own identity and goals. This book is intended to be representative, rather than comprehensive, in its analysis of the subject. That is, it examines the controversies spawned after Sept. 11th in three main case studies that represent the range of groups that can be considered "evangelical," along with snapshots of other churches, individuals and organizations that are engaging the issue. The second part of the book examines the coverage Muslims and Islam received in the evangelical press in the years before and after the attacks. Full disclosure: I wrote for *Christianity Today*, the main focus of the press report, as a freelance reporter during the late 1990s. My work with CT focused on bills appearing in the U.S. congress that were of interest to evangelicals.

A decade after Sept. 11, 2001 evangelicals fell into two primary camps with regard to Muslims. Some portrayed Islam as a form of evil, and Muslims as a direct theological and political threat. Others in the movement sought to develop relationships with Muslims that fostered constructive dialogue and deferred mission work under certain circumstances. While evangelicalism was formed as a somewhat unified response to modernism, the diverging responses to this new challenge calls into question the long-term cohesiveness of the movement.

1

INTRODUCTION TO AMERICAN EVANGELICALISM

"God, I hope it wasn't Muslims," Angela Miller said to herself when news broke of the terrorist attacks on September 11, 2001. Miller is an African-American woman who was working at a mosque in Northern Virginia at the time. She said that, as an American, the Sept. 11th attacks left her deeply saddened: "My heart sank, because everything that everyone else was feeling, I felt." As a Muslim, she feared a backlash against the religious community at the center of her life.[1]

More than 3,000 people died when hijacked passenger jets crashed into the World Trade Center towers, the Pentagon and the Pennsylvania countryside. A few short years after the attacks, the United States had toppled the hard-line Taliban regime in Afghanistan,

---

[1] Walter R. Ratliff, "Muslim Women After the Sept. 11th Attacks," Associated Press, 14 February 2002.

and was embroiled in a struggle to bring stability to post-Saddam Iraq in the heart of the Arab world.[2]

One effect of the Sept. 11th attacks inside the United States was a spike in interest in Islam and the Muslim world by evangelical Christians.[3] However, the way in which this interest manifested itself was not always positive for the American Muslim community. A report by the Council on American-Islamic Relations on the one-year anniversary of the attacks included a chapter called "Muslims Targeted by Extremism," citing numerous instances where fundamentalist and evangelical Christians, as well as politically conservative commentators, engaged in anti-Muslim rhetoric.[4]

For example, CAIR reported that during the June 2002 Southern Baptist Convention's annual gathering, a Jacksonville, Florida pastor called the Muhammad a "demon-possessed pedophile," and delivered a series of other comments that Muslims would find deeply offensive.[5]

Since the CAIR report came out, evangelical responses to Islam and Muslims have revealed fault lines not previously seen in the movement. In June 2003, during a 60 Minutes interview, Jerry Falwell referred to Muhammad as a terrorist.[6] A month prior to Falwell's remark, the president of the National Association of Evangelicals

---

[2] The Taliban are members of a fundamentalist Muslim movement in Afghanistan. The movement took control of much of the country in 1996, and allowed the Al Qaida movement to use the Afghanistan as a base for global terrorism training prior to Sept. 11, 2001.

[3] Norman Geisler and Abdul Saleeb, *Answering Islam*. In the preface to the book's second edition, the authors note that the 1993 edition of the book sold more than 42,000 copies. The authors say more than half of those sales were in the first two months after the Sept. 11, 2001 attacks.

[4] Mohamed Nimer, *American Muslims: One Year After 9-11*, 23-29. CAIR is a controversial Muslim human rights organization often criticized by evangelicals.

[5] Ibid., 23-24.

[6] Bob Simon, "Zion's Christian Soldiers," *60 Minutes*, 8 June 2003.

joined other religious leaders in condemning rhetoric that inflames tensions between Christians and Muslims.[7]

Over the past thirty years, evangelicals have become a powerful force on American religious and political scenes. Since their role in the election of Jimmy Carter in 1976, evangelicals have been cited as a major factor in politics, and have organized churchgoers in battles ranging from as abortion to foreign policy.

In the midst of the evangelicals' struggle to remain engaged in the broader culture, perceptions and actions within the movement are being molded by major events like Sept. 11th. Although the evangelical community had developed some responses to Islam and Muslims both in the U.S. and abroad prior to Sept. 11th, the attacks launched the issue of Christian-Muslim relations into the forefront of debate.

In 2003, Fuller Theological Seminary in Pasadena, California received a million-dollar grant from the U.S. Department of Justice to develop a controversial peacemaking program for Christians and Muslims. Around the same time, the National Association of Evangelicals and the Institute for Religion and Democracy called conferences and attempted to establish guidelines for evangelical-Muslim dialogue.[8] These initiatives were taking place even as well-known evangelical figures, including Franklin Graham, made remarks about Islam that Muslims found alarming.[9]

The variety in responses to Islam and Muslims by those within evangelicalism reflects the variety of thought within the movement itself. Some see the predicament evangelicals face over the course of

---

[7] Rachel Zoll, "Evangelical Leaders Condemn Anti-Islam Statements," Associated Press, 8 May 2003.

[8] Mark Stricherz, "Evangelicals Advise on Muslim Dialogue," *Christianity Today*, July 2003.

[9] Simon, "Zion's Christian Soldiers."

the 20th century as rising from nothing less than "the demise of the Church's institutional authority and clerical control."[10]

At the turn of the millennium, the Sept. 11th attacks forced the Christian world to not only deal with the pressures of modernity, but also a host of new theological, political and cultural challenges. Whereas theologically-conservative Christianity once primarily identified itself against secularism and theologically-liberal movements, the postmodern world presents challenges from other religions, alongside a variety of systems competing for legitimacy and adherents.

Recent books on the global phenomenon of fundamentalist reactions against the modern world often carry apocalyptic titles such as *The Battle for God*, and *Terror in the Mind of God*. However some intellectuals are thinking beyond the violent reactions of religious fundamentalists. These thinkers and activists are considering how religious communities can find elements in their own traditions that move them toward peaceful coexistence with those adhering to competing ideologies.

For example, Marc Gopin of George Mason University's Institute for Conflict Resolution and Analysis wrote a book (with the equally apocalyptic title: *Between Eden and Armageddon*) arguing that constructive, peaceful discourse can be developed within the framework of religiously conservative communities.[11] Gopin concentrates on building nonviolent, constructive conflict within Judaism.

Miroslav Volf stands at the forefront of evangelicals looking for theologically orthodox solutions to inter-religious conflict. Volf recognizes the tendency for Christians to withdraw from the world to strengthen and protect their identity as believers. He argues that this is

---

[10] Mark Juergensmeyer, *Terror in the Mind of God: The Global Rise of Religious Violence*, 229.

[11] Marc Gopin, *Between Eden and Armageddon: The Future of Religions, Violence and Peacemaking*, 8.

not the proper approach for Christians dealing with those outside the faith – just the opposite. He says biblical Christianity requires engagement. This includes representing the heart of Christianity to the parent culture as well as those that might be less familiar, including Muslims.[12] Volf, a Lutheran Croatian with a Pentecostal background, formed his outlook on the biblical response to his own and other cultures amid the violence of the early 1990's in the former Yugoslavia.

Even as Volf and others are developing methods for peaceful engagements with others of another culture and faith. However, the popular reception among evangelicals walks a line between militant opposition and constructive engagement.

Defining Evangelical

The first step in examining the dynamics of evangelical-Muslim relations is to explore the diverse set of communities that make up American evangelicalism. In fact, the movement's assortment of subgroups has prompted some to say the term "evangelical" has lost its meaning and should be discarded altogether. The term could refer to movements of sixteenth-century Reformationists, eighteenth-century Pietists as well as twentieth century fundamentalists. Among today's churches that fall under the evangelical category, big differences exist on issues such as eschatology, views of scripture and methods of worship. Disagreement among evangelical denominations on many key issues bolsters the argument against an umbrella term to cover the entire lot.[13]

However, the diversity that is encompassed by evangelicalism should instead be seen as a family resemblance, even though political and theological boundaries are not always clearly defined. Perhaps

---

[12] Miroslav Volf, *Exclusion and Embrace*.

[13] Donald W. Dayton, "Some Doubts About the Usefulness of the Category 'Evangelical,'" 245-251.

evangelicalism can be best seen as a fluid, organic model for gathering the various subsets into the movement's "family."[14]

The Institute for the Study of American Evangelicals at Wheaton College has constructed a three-fold way of viewing the evangelical movement:

1. The first is to view "evangelical" as all Christians who affirm a few key doctrines and practical emphases: conversionism; biblicism; and crucicentrism.

2. A second sense is to look at evangelicalism as an organic group of movements and religious tradition. Within this context "evangelical" denotes a style as much as a set of beliefs.

3. A third sense of the term is as the self-ascribed label for a coalition that arose during the Second World War. This group came into being as a reaction against the perceived anti-intellectual, separatist, belligerent nature of the fundamentalist movement in the 1920s and 1930s.[15]

A glance at the membership roster for the National Association of Evangelicals shows denominations ranging from the Salvation Army to the Fire Baptized Holiness Church of God of the Americas.[16] The NAE represents 43,000 churches with theological roots ranging from Reformed to Pentecostal to Anabaptist. Even so, the organization touts their mission as standing for "biblical truth ... and serving the evangelical community through united action, cooperative ministry, and strategic planning."[17]

---

[14] Robert K. Johnston, "American Evangelicalism: An Extended Family," 252-269.

[15] http://isae.wheaton.edu/defining-evangelicalism/defining-the-term-in-contemporary-times/

[16] National Association of Evangelicals list of member denominations: www.nae.net

[17] "Mission Statement," National Association of Evangelicals.

In an effort to cast a semantic net wide enough to cover the various groups that make up the movement, Alistar McGrath offers a definition of what constitutes an evangelical by applying four criteria related to the first set of criteria described above by the Wheaton College institute:

1. Conversionism: The "born-again" experience is emphasized based on the Bible passage from John 3:7. McGrath defines this as a "personal appropriation of faith."
2. Activism: McGrath defines this term as the actualization of Christian faith in life, with an emphasis on evangelism. He says: "One of the reasons evangelical churches are so successful is that their memberships tend to be very active in outreach and discipleship programs."
3. Biblicism: McGrath skips sometimes heated disputes over inerrancy and inspiration by defining this term as "a focus on the Bible as the most fundamental resource for Christian life and thought," and "Bible study is often at the heart of evangelical spiritual life."
4. Crucicentrism: McGrath defines this trait of evangelicalism as a "focus on the cross and the benefits it brings to humanity," namely atonement and salvation.[18]

The pollster George Barna reveals that 96 percent of American evangelicals describe themselves as "deeply spiritual," (in contrast to 61 percent of the general population), and are twice as likely to describe themselves as politically conservative as non-evangelicals. Barna also points out that evangelicals are often enthusiastically engaged in the public square: 88 percent are likely to vote. Among a spectrum of religious adherents, they have the strongest propensity for discussing issues of religion, politics and morality with others as well as for volunteering at church or for a Christian non-profit organization.[19]

---

[18] Alister E. McGrath, *The Future of Christianity*, 111-112.
[19] The Barna Group, "Evangelical Christians."

The Modern Evangelical Community

Key developments in the history contemporary evangelicalism include the establishment of the National Association of Evangelicals in 1942 by what historians have described as "a group of diverse conservatives who were dissatisfied with the politically-oriented and rabidly exclusivist" groups of churches organized in porevious years. By the time the leading evangelical publication *Christianity Today* was launched in 1956, the NAE claimed more than 1.5 million members. Most of the members were of the Pentecostal or Holiness variety, with the Assemblies of God, Church of God (Cleveland, Tenn.), National Association of Free Will Baptists and the Church of the Four Square Gospel making up two thirds of its total membership.[20]

From the late 1940's through the 1980's, the evangelical movement grew in numbers and organizational strength to become a major voice in the public arena. This period was marked by a decline in tensions between Protestants and Catholics, and between different Protestant denominations. One result of the decreased tension was that traditional organizations and denominational lines became less important as a generalized sense of common belief and mission between churches emerged. At the same time, para-church organizations without denominational ties began to proliferate.[21]

But as denominational diversity grew, so did tensions over the goals and beliefs that evangelicals were assumed to share. A person visiting individual evangelicals across the United States can find a host of assorted and often contradictory opinions on both politics and religion, depending on whether the person spoken to was from an urban center, a rural farmland, or a particular region. The broad pool labeled "American evangelicalism" reflects a varied landscape of agendas and outlooks.[22]

---

[20] Sydney Ahlstrom, *A Religious History of the American People*, 958.

[21] Robert Wuthnow, *The Struggle for America's Soul*, 16-17.

[22] Ibid., 179.

In broader terms, Protestantism in the U.S. has realigned along the liberal-conservative axis. Theologically-conservative Christianity left its predominantly Southern roots to become a national phenomenon, becoming a movement that has adapted itself to the needs of adherents in the wider culture. The spread of evangelicalism across social boundaries adapted to focus on individual needs of members, and has moved away from its role in pushing the American political and moral terrain toward its socially conservative values.[23] The more significant change in Protestantism than the liberal-conservative rift is the privatization of religion within evangelicalism, and therefore the "disestablishment" of the religious sector in civic life.[24]

If evangelicalism can be seen as a family of like-minded Christians, the varying theological and cultural environments created by its members can be seen as a variation on Jesus's parable of the sower:

> "A farmer went out to sow his seed. As he was scattering the seed, some fell along the path, and the birds came and ate it up. Some fell on rocky places, where it did not have much soil. It sprang up quickly, because the soil was shallow. But when the sun came up, the plants were scorched, and they withered because they had no root. Other seed fell among thorns, which grew up and choked the plants. Still other seed fell on good soil, where it produced a crop—a hundred, sixty or thirty times what was sown. He who has ears, let him hear." (Matthew 13:3-9 NIV)

Just as seeds take root in the soils they are best suited for, the ideas sowed throughout the evangelical community regarding interfaith relations may prosper in some social, theological and denominational terrain, but not in others. A look at some key features of that terrain relating to the subject at hand would aid in understanding where certain responses may thrive, and others wither.

---

[23] Mark A. Shibley, *Resurgent Evangelicalism in the United States*, 8.
[24] Ibid., 137.

The Sept. 11 attacks shook the cultural ground where evangelicals cultivate their view of themselves and their relationship to the rest of the world, bringing differences within the movement to the surface that were only hinted at before the attacks.

In order to understand the present challenges to evangelicalism it would be helpful to first examine a number of evangelical institutions that illustrate its diversity of character.

Southern Baptists and the "New Evangelicalism"

The history of the Southern Baptist Convention is a prime example a denomination forming their identity in response to the threat of modernism and theological liberalism. Baptist conservatives cultivating theological conservatism feared the weedy vetches of "liberal" scriptural interpretation and higher textual criticism - agents they feared would dilute their orthodox Christian identity. Understanding the background of the SBC shows how the liberal and secular value systems in the 20th century were seen as a clear danger to orthodoxy. The SBC's hostility to cooperation and understanding with Muslims in the post-Sept. 11th era seems to have been formed out of the battle within the denomination during the previous few decades.

The decades following World War Two saw American religious society splitting into distinct camps. Theologically-conservative Christians began to see secular humanism in schools and public policy as an imminent threat.[25]

Even after World War Two, self-declared fundamentalists were still trying to cope with the loss of the Northern mainline denominations that had traded a literal, inerrant view of the Bible for methods of higher criticism. The embarrassment of the Scopes trial in 1925 still loomed in the memory of many leaders.[26] The Tennessee

---

[25] Armstrong, 268.

[26] Mark Noll, *American Evangelical Christianity*, 16.

legal showdown over the teaching of evolution in public school, was the focal point in the effort to curtail the teaching of modern science in public schools. Leading up to the famous court battle, fundamentalists had waged a campaign to convince American Christians that science taught from the modernist perspective was incompatible with orthodox Christian beliefs, and therefore threatened to unravel to moral fabric of American society.[27]

Following the Scopes defeat, and before the arrival of the "New Evangelicals," the fundamentalists' primary reaction was to retreat from engagement with their theological enemies in the mainline denominations and their secular enemies in public schools and politics. As a result, tensions sprang up within large denominations such as the Southern Baptist Convention over the theological direction they were moving.

Southern Baptists split from their Northern brethren in the 1840's over objections to slavery. Calvinism characterized the predominant theology of the newly formed Southern denomination. However, some groups chafed against the centralizing tendencies of the SBC, and removed themselves from the organization over disagreements over Calvinist teachings such as free will and predestination.[28] Eventually, the SBC would grow to become the largest Protestant denomination in the United States.

In the 1930's the SBC's membership saw a 20 percent increase in membership, rising to more than 5 million members.[29] In the four years following World War Two, it grew by another 300,000 members.[30] Despite its size, the SBC became an intensely regional phenomenon. In nine southern states, 80-90 percent of the counties had a majority of Southern Baptists. By contrast, only 13 counties in 32 non-Southern

---

[27] Ahlstrom, 910.

[28] Noll, *A History of Christianity in the United States and Canada*, 179-180.

[29] Ibid., 432.

[30] Ibid., 437.

states had a majority of Southern Baptists. Even though the SBC is the largest Protestant denomination in the U.S., Baptists outside the SBC outnumber the ones inside the denomination.[31]

By contrast, membership in major liberal denominations declined in the decades following World War Two. Denominations such as the United Methodist Church, the United Church of Christ and the Presbyterian Church-USA were hemorrhaging members, whereas theologically conservative denominations such as the SBC, the Assemblies of God, and a host of non-denominational churches were seeing significant gains in attendance. Some scholars have characterized the divergent trends between mainline and conservative membership as a product of the liberal churches being less demanding doctrinally, while the conservative churches organized efforts to keep the church body centered on a firmly orthodox position.[32]

Beginning in the 1960's, fundamentalists within the SBC mobilized to counter what they saw as a drift in the denomination toward liberalism. One key effort was to organize votes to ensure the election of a conservative to the SBC presidency. With victories in this effort from 1979 onwards, the conservative influence in the denomination has trickled down through the appointment of board members and trustees in the vast denominational bureaucracy.[33]

As conservatives within the SBC began to secure the denomination's doctrine along fundamentalist/evangelical lines, those belonging to the church began to move politically to the right. In joining the "New Christian Right" of the 1980's, the SBC joined with other denominations that mixed pre-millennial eschatology and a view of America as a "new Zion" with conservative political activism.[34]

---

[31] Ibid., 472.

[32] Ronald B. Flowers, *Religion in Strange Times*, 40-41.

[33] Noll, *A History of Christianity*, 486.

[34] Martin E. Marty, "Fundamentalism as a Social Phenomenon," 315.

By 1997, the SBC had been sufficiently ensconced in the theologically conservative camp to satisfy the doctrinal and political concerns of one of the nation's most prominent evangelical political activists, Jerry Falwell. Falwell tied his participation as a voting member in the Convention directly to the triumph of the conservatives in the structure of the SBC: "All six of the seminaries now have biblical inerrantists as presidents. All the Southern Baptist agencies now are headed by inerrantists, and the thing that many of us thought never could happen— that is the return of the denomination to biblical authority—has happened."[35]

Religious scholars see Falwell as following the classic fundamentalist tendency to separate from society. As evidence, they point to the founding of his own college as well as setting up social services ranging from a home for alcoholics to an adoption agency that operated on theologically conservative principles.

Much academic literature tends to distinguish fundamentalists from those labeled "evangelical." However, some scholars note that many "in media, universities and government who attempt to interpret religious conservatism are scarcely able to distinguish a fundamentalist from an evangelical, let alone sort out the varieties of eschatological teaching or doctrines of biblical inspiration that conservatives may hold."[36]

Up until the Sept. 11th attacks, the primary threat felt by the Southern Baptist Convention, as well as activists like Jerry Falwell, was the influence of secular humanism in American education and politics. Falwell's Moral Majority was formed as a political organization to support conservative causes, as well as elect leaders in the public sphere. In some respects, this political movement paralleled theological

---

[35] David Winfrey, "Jerry Falwell Attends SBC, This Time as a Messenger," Associated Baptist Press, 11 June 1998.
[36] Ibid., 179.

conservatives' efforts within the Southern Baptist Convention during the last quarter of the 20th century to elect a fundamentalist/evangelical president of the SBC, and move the denomination toward religious conservatism. We shall see later how, after the Sept. 11th, attacks, the threat was transformed to include Muslims and the religion of Islam. SBC leadership saw the terrain of theological correctness as a hard-fought battleground, with little room for greater understanding of different interpretations of Christianity, much less other religions.

Lutheran Church - Missouri Synod

In December 1970, a young man in the Lutheran Church-Missouri Synod named Daniel Preus asked his father about attending the denomination's Concordia Seminary in St. Louis, Missouri. His father taught at the seminary, and he was looking forward to being close to his family after attending college in Ft. Wayne, Indiana. However, Prues's father told him, "Don't come here - not if you want a good Lutheran education. All you'll do is fight for your faith and you won't learn what you need to be a good pastor."[37]

It was a startling statement for the aspiring seminary student, but a clear indicator of the deep tensions facing the denomination as the contemporary theological divide between Christian conservatives and progressives was reaching maturity. Three years later, Daniel Preus's father, Jack, would lead a walkout by the majority of the faculty and students at the seminary. Soon, about 200,000 LCMS members would break away from the denomination to form the Association of Evangelical Lutherans.[38]

---

[37] Daniel Prues, "The Lutheran Church - Missouri Synod Holiday from History," 12-13.

[38] Ibid., 2.

Tensions over theological purity raged throughout the history of the Synod, from the denomination's earliest days through the aftermath of the Sept. 11th attacks. In the LCMS, like other theologically conservative denominations, the primary threat was seen as liberal biblical scholarship, and the theological implications that flow from it.

The LCMS is sometimes counted as an evangelical denomination, sometimes not. Strictly speaking, it falls into the category of "conservative confessional." However, the loose structure of evangelicalism encompasses the denomination's defining issues and beliefs, including biblical inerrancy. Also, the denomination's theological debates and positions on crucial public issues (such as gay marriage, interfaith relations, etc.) parallel the stances of modern evangelicalism so closely as to place the LCMS firmly in the evangelical family. Gene Edward Veith is a provost at Patrick Henry College, a former dean at LCMS's Concordia Theological Seminary and a culture editor at the prominent evangelical publication, *World Magazine*. He has described conservative confessional Lutherans, particularly those in his denomination, as a distinct branch of Christianity. He says they represent the best of the sacramental and evangelical worlds:

"Lutherans are starting to get their share of disaffected evangelicals—casualties of megachurches and refugees from generic American Protestantism, Christians looking for meaningful worship and theological depth—as well as Catholics dismayed by the post-Vatican II liberalism within their Church, and burnt-out secularists who, broken by the law and renewed by the gospel, have come to Christ," Veith wrote. "Many confessional Lutherans have taken to calling themselves "evangelical catholics." They are catholic in their historic creeds, their worship, and their sacramentalism, and they are evangelical in their trust in the good news of Christ, that in his cross he has saved us by sheer grace for a life of Christian freedom. Others are calling themselves 'confessing evangelicals,' allying with Reformed

Christians to call today's doctrinally shallow evangelicals to the historic confessions of faith forged by the Reformation."[39]

The LCMS was born out of an effort to preserve German Lutheran identity in the United States during the 19th century. The contemporary denomination is a product the denomination's ongoing effort to keep their conservatism and orthodoxy intact amid the transforming challenges of the modern world.

After the Civil War, the South looked toward old-style evangelicalism as a mark of identity and separateness from the wider American culture, replacing the political separateness that it had failed to achieve.[40] A century later, after the peak of fundamentalist backlash against modernism in first three decades of the twentieth century, conservative Protestantism was marginalized except in its Southern strongholds.[41]

In the 1840's, as Southern Baptists were on the verge of breaking ties with their co-religionists to the North, a group of young German immigrants set sail on five ships in hopes of starting a Lutheran colony in the United States. Their leader, Martin Stephan, preached a return to "old Lutheranism," which he saw as corrupted by his contemporaries from Germany to as far away as the United States.[42] After Stephan had suffered a series of arrests and false accusations, he and his followers selected Missouri as a new home where they could freely practice their style of Lutheranism.

What is now known as the Lutheran Church-Missouri Synod remained almost entirely a German-speaking denomination well into the twentieth century.[43] At first, the chief issue for the denomination

---

[39] Gene Edward Veith, "Evangelical Catholics & Confessional Evangelicals," *Touchtone Magazine*. May 1998.

[40] Shibley, 14.

[41] Ibid., 17.

[42] Eldon Weisheit, *The Zeal of His House*, 20.

[43] Ibid., 72, 91.

was its relationship with other Lutheran denominations in the U.S. and Canada. The division between the Lutheran bodies did not rest on doctrine, but practice. For example, the churches all spoke against membership in Freemasonry and other lodges, but not all required members to leave a lodge if they belonged to one. Also, all Lutheran groups upheld a belief in transubstantiation when taking communion, but not all Lutheran groups believed in closing their communion to those Christians who believed differently.[44]

As time went on, concern arose within the Synod over pastors who were holding fellowship with Lutherans who held differing doctrinal positions. In 1945, a document dubbed the "Statement of the 44" decried legalistic interpretations of scripture that were against fellowship with those at variance with Lutheranism as practiced within the LCMS. It was feared that the issues raised in the statement would lead to a split within the denomination, but the expected schism never occurred. However, the lasting contribution of the statement was an acknowledgment that there were deep internal tensions within the synod over its relationship to those outside its denominational boundaries.

Reaction to the "Statement," went beyond concerns over legalism and theological stagnation within the denomination. It also solidified the LCMS position as standing outside the ecumenical and theological movements of other mainline denominations, including other Lutherans.[45]

As other Lutheran denominations were adopting views of the Bible through the lens of modern scholarship's historical-critical approach, the LCMS struggled to find a place of unity with other Lutheran denominations. The denomination was also struggling internally over the issue of biblical inerrancy during the same period. Some historians say moderates in the denomination viewed critical approaches to scripture as helpful and acceptable, as long as one did

---

[44] Ibid., 93.

[45] Kurt E. Marquart, *Anatomy of an Explosion*, 12-15.

not accept the "radical anti-miracle bias of the wider principle." Others say the critical approaches to scripture were by their very nature incompatible with doctrinal views of scripture as inspired and inerrant.[46]

The simmering dispute reached a boiling point in 1973 during the New Orleans Convention. One controversial resolution condemned the teaching of the historical-critical method used by LCMS seminary professors, stating that modernist scholarship should "not be tolerated in the church of God, much less be excused and defended."[47] The subsequent walkout by the Concordia seminary faculty and students, and the split in the denomination, sealed the denomination's identity as staunchly conservative both in doctrine and practice.

Challenges before and after Sept. 11, 2001 continued to test the denomination's resolve and unity. A protectionist culture within the denomination has made the terrain of LCMS almost completely barren toward interfaith relations, where seeds of constructive dialogue would likely not take root. However, some of those within the denomination have seen outcroppings of biblical doctrine that allow for clergy participation in some interfaith contexts without compromising their own identity and orthodoxy. The involvement of an LCMS pastor in a New York interfaith prayer service after Sept. 11th, and the heresy charges that followed, reveal ongoing tensions springing from within the denomination.

Fuller Theological Seminary

A key institution that has become a meeting ground, and sometimes a battleground, for the various streams of evangelicalism is Fuller Theological Seminary in Pasadena, California. The background of the institution shows how, in the pre-Sept. 11-era, the school

---

[46] Ibid., 122-123.
[47] Prues, 9.

creatively dealt with the challenges to evangelical orthodoxy, which in turn created a terrain much friendlier to interfaith relations.

The roots of the seminary reach back to 1937 when Charles E. Fuller began a radio program called the "Old Fashioned Revival Hour." The popularity of Fuller's radio show grew quickly on the CBS radio network, reaching an audience of about 10 million within two years of it going on the air.[48]

In the years prior to World War Two, the "new evangelical" movement had yet to spring out of the fundamentalist milieu. However, Charles Fuller and others such as Harold Ockenga had discussed moving beyond the separatism and intellectual withdrawal that characterized conservative Christianity in the years following the Scopes trial.

In 1942, Ockenga had helped found the National Association of Evangelicals as a response to Carl MacIntire's fundamentalist American Council of Christian Churches. In the years that followed, he teamed up with Charles Fuller to found the seminary. Fuller's vision for the school was a classic evangelical response to both the threat of modernism that came from mainline denominations, and an answer to the antagonism to modernity found among fundamentalists. The radio preacher hoped that, with the help of some of the nation's most prominent evangelical scholars, he could open what would become the "Cal-Tech of modern evangelicalism."[49]

A tide of new evangelicalism was rising across the country when Fuller was founded. Thriving Pentecostal and holiness churches were being courted by the NAE, Billy Graham was beginning his phenomenally popular revival tours around the country, and older, theologically conservative strongholds such as Wheaton College and Moody Bible Institute were experiencing a surge in enrollment.

---

[48] Noll, *History of Christianity*, 432.
[49] Christian Smith, *American Evangelicalism: Embattled and Thriving*, 11.

Though Fuller was founding a seminary that would counter the cultural divisiveness and anti-intellectualism of fundamentalism, Charles Fuller had much in common doctrinally with the movement. One prominent feature of fundamentalism, and Fuller's theology, was dispensationalist eschatology.[50]

Dispensationalist Theology

John Nelson Darby first mapped out the dispensationalist system in the mid-nineteenth century. Darby's view of the end times was that Christ would rescue the world's true Christians just before seven years of tribulation would strike the earth. Following the tribulation, the Church would return with Christ to build the millennial Kingdom of God.[51]

One feature of Darby's system is that it introduced the reestablishment of the state of Israel as an integral part of the end-time scenario. It also introduced a vision of history based upon periods of time, or "dispensations." The final stage before the return of Christ was the Church age, a "historical parenthesis" where the church is called to remove itself from ungodliness, evangelize the world and prepare for the final days.[52]

Dispensationalism infused itself deeply into fundamentalism by the 1930's, and became viewed by many as orthodox and authoritative as the inerrancy of scripture. Though many fundamentalists and evangelicals may not recognize Darby's name, most would recognize the Scofield Reference Bible published by Oxford University Press. The Scofield Bible has transmitted Darby's eschatological ideas to a wide audience during much of the twentieth century. Some students at the time parodied a popular hymn to capture the deep influence of

---

[50] George Marsden, *Reforming Fundamentalism*, 20.
[51] Ahlstrom, 809.
[52] Noll, *A History of Christianity*, 377.

dispensationalism on fundamentalist and evangelical Christianity: "Our hope is built on nothing less/Than Scofield's notes and Moody Press."[53]

Darby's theology of dispensationalism, though it has gone through some adjustments, has had a lasting and popular influence in some sectors of fundamentalist and evangelical Christianity. The cataclysmic predictions of the system have captured the popular imagination from time to time, as evidenced in the phenomenal popularity of Hal Lindsay's book *The Late Great Planet Earth*, published in 1970. At the turn of the millennium, the *Left Behind* series of novels by Tim LaHaye and Jerry Jenkins spawned a small industry of books, study guides, movies, a "prophecy club" newsletter, music compilations, and even a video game rooted largely in Darby's eschatological framework.[54]

More recently, the *Last Jihad* series of novels and the nonfiction work by evangelical conservative political activist Joel C. Rosenberg have continued the tradition of literature focusing on dispensationalist theology.

A key feature of dispensationalism is role of Israel. The establishment of the nation in 1948 was seen by most dispensationalists as a fulfillment of prophecy, and a requirement for the return of Christ. Today, many evangelical Christians support pro-Israel candidates, and help fund the migration of Jews to the nation because of the role Israel plays in their beliefs about the end-times.[55]

In George Marsden's book on the history of Fuller Seminary, he describes Christians adhering to dispensationalism as believing that "civilization was beyond repair and Christians could only preach the gospel, hope to rescue the perishing, keep themselves pure, and wait for the coming King."[56] A more optimistic view of the Church's role in

---

[53] Timothy P. Weber, "Premillenialism and the Branches of Evangelicalism," 15.

[54] http://www.leftbehind.com

[55] Simon.

[56] Marsden, 75.

society was one feature of evangelicalism that the founders of Fuller Seminary hoped to revive. Harold Ockenga characterized the virtues of engagement versus the perils of fundamentalist separatism in a convocation during the early days of the seminary:

> What I have said about Germany in its intellectual development could be repeated out of the teachings of the leading educators of America in this day. Here comes the message to America - America, which is experiencing today that inner rupture of its character and culture, that inner division with vast multitudes of our people following that secularist, rationalist lie of scientific naturalism in the repudiation of God and God's law. I tell you on the authority of the Word of God and with the full sweep of history behind us that in the proportion that America does that, and the church has to withdraw itself to a separated community again, and there enters a time of hostility of the world and the persecution of the anti-Christian forces, in that percentage we will open ourselves up to the kind of judgment that God brought upon Europe from which we escaped almost unscathed in this nation.[57]

Ockenga argued that evangelical theology was commissioned with nothing less than redeeming Western culture. Marsden regards this intellectual effort as "direct repudiation of the dispensationalist church as a refuge in a ruined culture, and a Calvinist-Puritan view that the church must play a central civilization building role."[58]

In contrast to the Lutheran Church-Missouri Synod's cautious approach toward fellowship with those who believe or practice their faith differently, Fuller Seminary moved to embrace the diversity of beliefs that fall under evangelicalism. Edward Carnell, who assumed the seminary's presidency in 1955, said in his inaugural address that the "crowning glory" of the seminary was "an attitude of tolerance and

---

[57] Ibid., 63.
[58] Ibid.

forgiveness toward individuals whose doctrinal convictions are at variance with those that inhere in the institution itself."[59]

Some on the faculty reacted sharply to talk of Carnell's talk of tolerance, saying it resembled the ecumenism and modernism of the mainline denominations that they were trying to protect themselves from. Carnell continued to come under pressure from those who were threatened by his views of tolerance within the seminary, and resigned in 1959. Outside Fuller Seminary, similar tensions were occurring between evangelicals and fundamentalists who were demanding a separatist approach. The prime example of this was the split between fundamentalists and evangelist Billy Graham.

Since the late-1940's Graham had gained notoriety for his revival meetings, and was noted for his use of mass marketing through radio, television and print to draw people to his crusades. In an effort to create ties with local churches, he enlisted local congregations in planning the revivals and following up on those who attended. The split between Graham and fundamentalists occurred in 1957, when Graham enlisted the support of mainline, non-evangelical denominations in his crusades. Fundamentalists could not bear that Graham allowed new converts to be steered toward churches with liberal theologies.[60]

Though the short-lived presidency of Carnell caused some discomfort among the most conservative players at Fuller Seminary, the biggest battle came in December 1962. In a day that became known as "Black Saturday," an argument over the election of the seminary's president erupted between the strict conservatives among the seminary's officers and the "progressives." At the core of the dispute was a fight over the use of higher criticism and the nature of biblical inerrancy. Each side was concerned how the winner of the debate could define the seminary's teaching over the long-term. The debate was, in essence, over the same issues that spawned the walkout at

---

[59] Ibid., 148.

[60] Noll, *History of Christianity*, 511.

Concordia Seminary and the split in the Lutheran Church-Missouri Synod a dozen years later.[61]

Leading one side of the debate was Ockenga, the conservative cofounder of the seminary who opposed any admission that the Bible contained inaccuracies. Leading the "progressives" was Dan Fuller, the son of the seminary's namesake. The school was debating the selection of the scholar David Hubbard, whose commitment to biblical inerrancy and rejection of historical criticism had come into question. Following the "Black Saturday" outbursts during a planning meeting for the seminary, the two sides became embroiled in a struggle over both political control over the seminary and academic control over defining the nature scripture. At one point, the conservatives tried to counter Dan Fuller's influence over the process by bringing in Billy Graham, who had been on the search committee, as an advocate for an alternative choice for seminary president.[62]

Despite Graham's intervention, Hubbard was installed as Fuller's president. The resulting fallout was that many of the more conservative/fundamentalist members of the faculty resigned. Also, Marsden notes that the concern over the seminary's theological direction also cost Charles Fuller's "Old Fashioned Revival Hour" about 40 percent of its support, and resulted in two trustees leaving the seminary board.[63]

As a matter of perspective, it should be noted that although the conservative/progressive dispute over scriptural inerrancy rankled those opposed to higher criticism, the actual dispute never approached the level of theological disagreement that evangelicals and fundamentalists had with mainline and liberal seminaries. The chief concern, voiced by Harold Lindsell after leaving the seminary's faculty,

---

[61] Marsden, 208.

[62] Ibid., 218.

[63] Ibid., 223.

was that "once inerrancy goes, it leads, however slowly, to a further denial of other biblical truths."[64]

From 1963 onward, Fuller Seminary became the chief institution for the moderate wing of American evangelicalism. Just as the neo-evangelicals of the 1950's had defined themselves against the fundamentalists, the post-1963 Fuller evangelicals were open to broader alliances. In the words of George Marsden, the result was that "some of the old guard of conservative neo-evangelicalism were now beginning to play the role that fundamentalists had played in the seminary's early days."[65]

As a result of these controversies, commitment to biblical inerrancy at the seminary dropped, and that by 1982 only about 15 percent of students held that view. Also, whereas the roots of the seminary were in Presbyterianism, along with Baptist and Calvinist streams of evangelicalism, by the 1980's nearly half of the students considered themselves Pentecostal or charismatic. The seminary's open stance toward all streams of evangelicalism had made it place where a more representative sampling of American conservative Christianity could be found on campus.[66]

This survey of Fuller's history has shown how views regarding the outside challenges to evangelicalism were transformed as the old guard with fundamentalist tendencies lost their influence, leaving evangelical moderates to shape the ideological direction of the school. By gaining leadership at Fuller, the new guard would seek engagement with other members of the evangelical family, with less of an emphasis on protecting a limited theological or cultural worldview.

In the decades before Sept. 11, 2001, Fuller rode the crest of the evangelical wave where tendencies of protection and isolation were overcome by the younger evangelicals' desire for greater engagement.

---

[64] Robert Booth Fowler, *A New Engagement*, 25.

[65] Marsden, 256.

[66] Ibid., 269.

That desire for constructive engagement across theological boundaries would help set the stage in the post-Sept. 11 era for a project designed to break down animosity between Christians and Muslims.

While other evangelical institutions were emphasizing protection, Fuller was using what sociologists Robert Benford and David Snow would define as "frame amplification" to instill openness and dialogue (within certain limits) among different streams of Christianity.[67] Those values instilled by Fuller's leadership can be seen as the basis for extending that "frame" of dialogue and understanding into a context that crossed religious boundaries as well.

In the past fifty years, evangelicalism has struggled to define itself against protectionist fundamentalism, yet remain orthodox in the face of the theological liberalism found among the mainline denominations. In the Southern Baptist Convention, the Lutheran Church - Missouri Synod, and Fuller Theological Seminary battles have been fought over what exactly it means to be evangelical in relation to modernity. The issues in each case were composed of struggles over institutional and political control, as well as debates over scriptural inerrancy and higher criticism in biblical scholarship.

In the 1960's, the "progressives" moved Fuller Seminary into a position that allowed a more moderate manifestation of evangelicalism. In the 1970's, conservatives were able to effectively organize campaigns to move denominations, such as the SBC and LCMS, into the more conservative wing of the movement. By 1976, with the election of Jimmy Carter as president, evangelicals were recognized as a political force to be reckoned with.[68] In the 1980's the movement produced evangelical political institutions such as Falwell's Moral Majority, and has come to play an increasingly important role on the political scene.

---

[67] Robert D. Benford, David A. Snow, "Framing Processes and Social Movements," 615.

[68] Fowler, 227.

So far, the discourse of how an evangelical is defined has rested on the continuum of the conservative theological response to modernism. Stands made over biblical inerrancy are a prime example. From the 1940's until recently, identity challenges among evangelical institutions have not, outside of missiological concerns, delved deeply into theological and social responses to other religions.

After Sept. 11th, the environment shifted from challenges of primarily liberalism and secularism, to diverse theological and social values among other religions and systems. Though the challenges outside the evangelical world may change, evangelicals often show how their responses are rooted in past conflicts and challenges, including their responses to Islam and Muslims in recent years.

WALTER R. RATLIFF

2
EVANGELICAL DISCOURSE TOWARD MUSLIMS: THREE CASES

In 2003, the Ethics and Public Policy Center conservative think tank in Washington DC released a poll on evangelical views of Islam. The results showed an overwhelmingly unfavorable view toward Islam (77 percent). A number of other indicators illustrated a growing rift between the two religious communities.[69]

Among most questions, the poll results showed very little ambiguity in evangelical attitudes. For example, when it came to the issues of conversion and the truth of the Gospel, almost all evangelicals supported these central tenets of the group's identity. On the other hand, more than 70 percent of evangelicals agreed with statements such as: Islam opposes religious freedom, Islam opposes pluralism/democracy, Shariah violates human rights, and Islam is a

---

[69] "Evangelical Views of Islam," Ethics and Public Policy Center/Beliefnet, 7 April 2003.

religion of violence. Additionally, seventy-nine percent disagreed with the idea that Muslims and Christians prayed to the same God.[70]

However, on some issues, the opinions of the evangelical community were not as monolithic. On the question whether the "war against terrorism is basically a war between the West and Islam," the results showed evangelicals evenly split at 45 percent. Also, just over half of evangelicals agreed that Islam preaches justice and moral values.[71]

On the issue of evangelical-Muslim relations, the poll showed most evangelicals were favorable. For example, 79 percent said it was "very important" to protect the rights of Muslims (with 20 percent saying it had "some importance"). Also, 54 percent of evangelicals said dialogue with Muslims was "very important," (41 percent answered it was of "some importance"). A nearly equal portion of the evangelical community said it was important to welcome Muslims into the American community.[72]

The survey painted a picture of the evangelical family divided between its own sentiments toward Muslims, and the courses of action to take toward this community.

Returning to the metaphor of the "family farm," each segment of the evangelical movement offered different "crops" of interpretation, and criticized how other members were tending their ideological fields. Each member contended they remained inside the fence when it came to evangelical theology and commitment to purpose. However, some fellow evangelicals were quick to point out when they believed others have drawn the wrong boundaries in the effort to build positive relationships with, or distance themselves from, Muslims.

---

[70] Ibid.

[71] Ibid.

[72] Ibid.

Southern Baptist Convention: Cultivating Polemics

As the Southern Baptist Convention grew more theologically conservative, leaders and activists such as Jerry Falwell rejoined the denomination, regarding it as having returned sufficiently to Protestant orthodoxy. From the 1970's through the 1990's the SBC also extended its influence into the political arena, transforming the denomination's fundamentalist tendencies into a system of evangelical engagement in the public square.

Former SBC president Jerry Vines joined the list of names (including Falwell, Pat Robertson and Franklin Graham) commonly grouped together by Muslim critics of evangelicals. Vines' called the prophet Muhammad as a "demon-possessed pedophile" in June 2002.[73] This helped renew the controversy over evangelical rhetoric toward Muslim after Sept. 11, 2001.

The remarks by Vines and others are merely a product of some of the deeper trends within the SBC. (For example, Vines' remarks were drawn from a book by Emir and Ergun Caner, which show the undercurrent of influence the brothers have within the denomination.) The anti-Muslim rhetoric of Southern Baptists such as former SBC president Jerry Vines and Rev. Jerry Falwell were well documented as a source of conflict within evangelicalism in the previous chapter. However, those remarks sparked dissent between members of the SBC and their cousins in the evangelical family. For example, the National Association of Evangelicals and the Institute for Religion and Democracy held a "consultation on evangelical Christian-Muslim Relations," in which they condemned the rhetoric by Franklin Graham and others, and issued a set of guidelines for Muslim-Christian interaction.

---

[73] Alan Cooperman, "Anti-Muslim Remarks Stir Tempest" *Washington Post, 20* .June 2002, A03.

In an open letter, IRD president Dianne Knippers praised the work of Graham's organization, Samaritan's Purse, in places such as southern Sudan. However, she told him that calling Islam "evil" and "wicked" has damaged the credibility of his work in the Muslim world among non-evangelicals, and has drawn fire from some quarters when he was invited to speak at a Good Friday service at the Pentagon. Knippers presented Graham with the idea that American Muslims could find common cause with Christians seeking to ensure the place of religion in the public square.[74]

Although he was not mentioned by name in the NAE and IRD's "loving rebuke" of fiery rhetoric by evangelicals, Jerry Falwell took issue with the comments made by NAE President Ted Haggard at the consultation. Haggard is quoted in Falwell's response as saying, ""Since we are in a global community, no doubt about it, we must temper our speech and we must communicate primarily through actions."[75]

Falwell responded by accusing NAE executives of "perhaps craving a bit of the national spotlight," and taking issue with the word "rebuke" to describe the Haggard's position. "Clearly, their intent was to slam everyone who has criticized Islam and pat themselves on the back for taking their own designation of the high road," Falwell wrote. In the letter, Falwell committed to "being more sensitive in his personal remarks about the followers of Islam," but disagreed with the portrayal of Islam as a peaceful religion in the face of attacks by Islamist militants.[76]

Though Falwell complained that he was merely being blamed for bad behavior by those caught up in the "political correctness" of offering only kind words for Islam, he credited the NAE for remaining true to evangelical tenets of exclusivity and conversion: "Thankfully,

---

[74] Dianne Knippers, "Letter to Franklin Graham," 19 May 2003.

[75] Jerry Falwell, "First Person," Baptist Press, 27 May 2003.

[76] Ibid.

NAE officials also reiterated their commitment to witnessing in the Muslim world and criticized the "naive" approach of the World Council of Churches, which has attempted to blur theological lines in its efforts of inclusion."

In Falwell's letter, he also quotes an email from former SBC president Jerry Vines to Haggard. Vines is quoted as disagreeing with the manner in which the rebuke was delivered, and whether a rebuke was necessary at all: "Rebuke' is a pretty strong word. As I understand it, personal sin must be involved before a rebuke is issued. I would like for you to point out to me what my sin was for which you issued me a 'loving rebuke.'"[77]

During the months following the IRD and NAE's "consultation," the challenge of Islam reached further into the seminaries and intellectual leaders of the denomination. In Spring 2004, one year after the "consultation" and response by Falwell and Vines, the SBC was ready to deliver a more comprehensive answer to Islam and Muslims than had been reflected in previous rhetoric. A special issue of the Southern Baptist Journal of Theology was devoted to defining Islam against Christianity, articulating the SBC's view of the nature of interfaith relations with Muslims. This issue of the journal is a prime example of the SBC's interest in the "threat" posed by Islam and the question of what the post-9/11 world means for evangelical-Muslim relations.

In the issue's lead editorial, Dr. Stephen J. Wellum of the Southern Baptist Theological Seminary wrote, "From the perspective of Scripture, Muslims require not only our understanding and dialogue but out fervent prayers and gospel witness." The journal articles generally presented the challenge of Islam as follows:

a) The religion is uniform in its orthodox beliefs about culture, political systems and relationships with those outside Islam.

---

[77] Ibid.

b) Woven throughout the religion itself are veins of militarism and the approved use of force to advance Islam.

c) Islamic theology is "alien" to Christianity in its fundamental teachings on the nature of God and His relationship with humanity.

Given those foundational assumptions in the journal, there are a few mentions of diversity of beliefs and attitudes among Muslims. One notable exception came from D.A. Carson. The prominent evangelical theologian argued that the first thing Christians must understand is that "in its own way, Islam is as varied as the world of Christendom."

"Muslims may vociferously disavow and condemn the views of many other Muslims," Carson wrote. "There is a distinction between the well-informed Muslim (of whatever group) and what for lack of a better expression we might call the street Muslim," who has a thin grasp of Islam's key teachings as well as misunderstandings about Christianity. Outside of Carson's analysis, most authors in the journal painted Islam and the Muslim community with a broad brush, suggesting homogeneity among Islamic ideologies and interpretations of the Quran around the world.

However, Chad Owen Brand countered this argument. He pointed to Sayyid Qutb as an activist and thinker that defined Western civilization as driving "a wedge between God and culture," which can only be remedied by resisting Western ways in their entirety, "including engaging in war and acts of sabotage and terrorism."[78] Brand saw Qutb's vision as the defining ideology of most in the Muslim world.

"Evangelicals have also been on the forefront in denouncing the evidences of decay of the Western tradition that seem to abound in our time," Brand argues, "But thoughtful westerners will realize that the Islamic solution to the cultural problem is a chimera, and one that

---

[78] Chad Owen Brand, "As Far as the East is From the West," 9.

holds promise for only those who are inclined to accept all of the tenets of Islam."[79]

Brand also noted: "Mutual respect is needed [between Christians and Muslims], but such seems unlikely to be mutual any time soon, given the current state of temper in the Islamic world."[80]

Emir Fethi Caner and Ergun Mehmet Caner, former Sunni Muslims who converted to Christianity in 1982 and 1983, penned an article on the doctrine of jihad in the Southern Baptist Journal of Theology. The Caner brothers' ideas about Muhammad came to the forefront of evangelical-Muslim discourse in 2002 when former SBC president Jerry Vines quoted their book *Unveiling Islam* in describing Muhammad as a "demon-possessed pedophile."[81]

The Caner brothers argued their "central thesis that Islam does in fact have an essential and indispensable tenet of militaristic conquest at its heart."[82] The Caners present Islam as not only a competing religious ideology, but also a faith that specifically targets Christians and Muslim converts to Christianity for violence: "Christianity is a specific enemy of Islam, and, thus, held out for specific scorn in the Quran."[83] However, The Caners do not balance this portrayal with other Quranic passages that encourage tolerance and friendship with Christians, including Surah 5:82: "Thou wilt find the nearest in friendship to the believers who say, 'We are Christians.'"[84]

The Caners argued that Muslims have an inherent insecurity about their salvation. They assert that, in Islam, martyrdom is the only sure

---

[79] Ibid.

[80] Ibid., 10.

[81] Todd Stames, "Southern Baptist Leaders Affirm Vines in Wake of National Attacks," *Baptist Press*, 19 June 2002.

[82] Emir F. Caner and Ergun M. Caner, "The Doctrine of Jihad in the Islamic Hadith," 33.

[83] Ibid., 36.

[84] Maulana Muhammad Ali, trans., *The Holy Quran*, 272.

way to heaven, creating a source of terrorism within Islam itself. "Since Allah is completely removed from his people and is in no way incarnational or personal, " the Caners wrote, "the [Sept. 11] terrorists followed the dastardly route imposed upon them by the only sources they could trust and that guaranteed them paradise: the literal rendering of the Hadith and Quran."[85]

The influence of the Caners in contemporary evangelical discourse was severely damaged after a controversy erupted surrounding statements Ergun Caner made about his Muslim past. An alliance of Muslim and Christian bloggers revealed inconsistencies about Ergun Caner's claim that he grew up in a climate of Muslim extremism in Turkey, as well as claims that he had debated a number of prominent Muslim scholars. As a result, Liberty University removed Caner as dean of the school's seminary but kept him on as a faculty member for one more year.[86] In 2011, he took a position at Arlington Baptist College, a small school not affiliated with the Southern Baptist Convention. Emir Caner, not implicated in the controversy, remained president of Truett-McConnell College, a small Southern Baptist institution in Georgia.

Evangelical scholars Norman Geisler and Amar Djaballah also wrote on the nature of Jesus in the Quran, comparing it to what is presented in the New Testament. Djaballah argued that understanding of Jesus in Christianity is much closer to how Muslims view the Quran. That is, each are regarded in Islam and Christianity as the Word sent directly from God, and that there is a fundamental difference in who Jesus is between Christians and Muslims. He asks, "What do Christians find distinctive in the teaching of the New Testament? In a sentence — God is in Christ reconciling the world to Himself."[87]

In bolstering his argument against Islamic theology, Djaballah quotes Kenneth Cragg: "In Islam, that which 'associates' God with

[85] Ibid., 40.
[86] William Wan and Michelle Boorstein, "Liberty U. Removing Ergun Caner as Seminary Dean Over Contradictory Statements," *Washington Post*, June 30, 2010.
[87] Amar Djaballah, "Jesus in Islam," 26.

humanity is prophethood, and supremely the prophethood of Muhammad. The Christian faith has the same trust in God's 'relationally' to man but locates it finally and inclusively in Jesus – in Jesus not simply as the spokesman of a message, but also as the 'event of grace' in which divine love is known in action."[88]

Geisler expands on this comparison of Jesus as the central figure of Christianity by contrasting it with Muhammad's role in Islam. He sums up the comparison by pointing out, "According to the Quran, Jesus was sinless and Muhammad was not. Jesus was virgin born, and Muhammad was not. Jesus was called 'Messiah,' and Muhammad was not," and so on. Furthermore, Geisler questions that authority by which Muhammad takes the cloak of prophethood: "On the one hand, we have Muhammad who at first believed he was demon-possessed and was later talked out of it by the *voice of his wife* [emphasis his] who was no doubt ambitious for her husband's success. On the other hand we have Jesus who knows from the beginning where he came from (Luke 2:49; cf. John 17:5) and who was later confirmed three times to be the Son of God by the *voice of God* (Matt: 3:17; John 12:28)."[89]

D.A. Carson, who was mentioned earlier for noting the diversity of Islam, portrayed Muslim arguments against Christianity and the West as often having a selective view of history, especially with regard to Muslim violence and the use of force against Christians. Carson argued that while Muslims point to the Crusades and colonialism, they often ignore the military expansion of Islam as far as Europe in the early Muslim empire, and the ongoing violence against Christians in places such as Nigeria and Indonesia.[90]

Carson also argued that Christians need to understand differences in how Christians and Muslims understand salvation, and how that understanding creates a theological gulf between the two faiths. He

---

[88] Ibid.

[89] Norman L. Geisler: "Jesus and Muhammad in the Quran," 58.

[90] Carson, et. al., 91-92.

cited an example of a Thai Muslim belief that reading the Quran in Arabic, but not understanding the words, will earn "extra credit" with God, while reading a translation of the Quran earns nothing.[91]

"Contrast this with the importance of intelligibility in Paul's estimate of things (1 Corinthians 14)," Carson wrote, "If by hearing the Word we have faith, if by knowing the truth we are set free, if by grace through faith we are saved, then from a biblical perspective Islam is a profoundly alien religion. Understand this, weep, and evangelize."[92]

Though other members of the evangelical family called for working with Muslims in common interests such as religious liberty, the SBC seemed to have planted the roots of division even deeper by laying out a vision of Islam as irrational, monolithic, and geared toward violence. However, not all Baptists share these views.

Dr. Glen Stassen, who teaches ethics at Fuller Seminary and is a recent president of the National Association of Baptist Professors of Religion, maintains Baptist tolerance and advocacy for religious liberty, even to Muslims, reaches to the earliest days of the movement.

"The original Baptists in the 1600's in England, the very first Baptists, you know, were battling for religious liberty," Stassen said, "and they were battling for religious liberty for Baptists, and Presbyterians, and Catholics, and Jews and Turks. And by [Turks] they meant Muslims. This is true of the first comprehensive writer of human rights theory, Richard Overton [1642-63], a Baptist, and also Roger Williams, founder of Rhode Island [and the first Baptist church in America in 1638] and so on. They both wrote about religious liberty for Turks, right from the beginning of Baptist life on. Kind of proud of that."[93]

---

[91] Ibid., 94-95.

[92] Ibid.

[93] Glen H. Stassen, interview by author, 29 September 2004.

Stassen, affiliated with the American Baptist denomination, regards Falwell's stance on Islam as a reversion to a "fundamentalist" position, rather than a true part of evangelical tradition. Though Stassen and others see theological and cultural polemics dominating Southern Baptist Convention discourse toward Islam and Muslims, there were important instances of a more sober and balanced approach in the wake of the Sept. 11 attacks and in the years that followed. One example was a letter issued in October 2001, which was signed by the current SBC president, Dr. James Merritt, along with the evangelical luminaries such as Campus Crusade founder Bill Bright, Focus on the Families' Dr. James Dobson, Assemblies of God General Superintendent Dr. Thomas Trask, and Pat Robertson.

The letter suggested several biblical responses to the attacks on New York and Washington, DC, including a call for repentance, calling the attacks a "reflection of the crumbling foundation of America." The joint letter summed up the response by saying: "The atrocities committed by fanatics must not be allowed to shape our attitudes towards people of other nationalities or religions, most of whom are as appalled by what has happened as we are. In these uncertain times, we must respond by faith, not fear; in hope, not despair; with love, not hate; with humility, not pride; with action, not apathy."[94]

A group called the Baptist Peace Fellowship, not affiliated with the SBC, released a "Peace Primer" in conjunction with another group calling itself the Muslim Peace Fellowship. The goal of the 44-page pamphlet was to give mediators involved in Muslim-Christian conflict resolution a way to listen to what scripture and tradition has to say regarding efforts to make peace with those outside their own faith.[95]

The pamphlet urged Muslims to "help contestants clarify their principles, and hold them to the principles they profess, backing this up with Surah 5:48, "If Allah had so willed He would have made you all

---

[94] James O. Davis, "A Biblical Response to America's Emergency," October 2001.
[95] Ken Shehested and Rabia Terri Harris, *Peace Primer*.

one community but [He wishes] to test you in that which he has given you, so compete with each other in good works."

It also quotes *ahadith* that encourage justice and tolerance, including "That man whose neighbor is not safe from harassment has no faith. (Bukhari and Muslim);" and "A strong person is not the person who throws his adversaries to the ground. A strong person is the one who contains himself when he is angry. (*al-Muwatta*)"[96]

The primer also lists "twelve things every Christian should know" about the pursuit of peace, including assertions that peace is the will of God, the fruit of the Spirit is peace, peacemaking is rooted in grace, and the foundation of peace is justice. Under each item, the authors list a series of scripture references. For example, under the point "Peace was the mission of Jesus," it listed "Jesus' role as the 'Prince of Peace' was foretold by Isaiah (9:6). Angels announcing the birth declared 'Glory to God' and 'peace on earth' (Lk. 2:14). Weeping over Jerusalem, Jesus prayed: 'would that you knew the things that make for peace.' (Lk. 19:41-42)."[97]

The primer also quotes a range of comments on peacemaking from Christian tradition, from the early church to the 20th Century:

> Now the trumpet sounds with a mighty voice calling the soldiers of the world to arms, announcing war. And shall not Christ, who has uttered his summons to peace even to the ends of the earth, summon together his own soldiers of peace? Indeed, O man, he has called to arms with his Blood and his Word an army that sheds no blood. To these soldiers he has handed over the Kingdom of Heaven... *Clement of Alexandria (c.150-c.215)*[98]

---

[96] Ibid., *13*.
[97] Ibid., 21.
[98] Ibid., 29.

The ultimate weakness of violence is that it is a descending spiral begetting the very thing it seeks to destroy. Instead of diminishing evil, it multiplies it. Through violence you murder the hater, but you do not murder hate. In fact, violence merely increases hate. Returning violence for violence multiplies violence, adding deeper darkness to a night already void of stars. *Martin Luther King Jr.*[99]

The booklet encourages Muslim and Christian believers to build bridges between the two communities, using the *Primer* as an educational tool and a starting point for dialogue. It also suggested reaching across religious boundaries during major festivals and holidays "for a meal and educational presentation."[100]

The LCMS and the Benke Controversy

"Allahu Akbar," rang the clear, melodic voice of Abdul Wali Y. Shaheed through Yankee Stadium twelve days after the Sept. 11 attacks, "Ash hadu alla ilaha illa-llah."[101] A few minutes later Imam Izak-El M. Pasha, a Muslim chaplain in the New York City Police Department, stood before the crowd wearing a tan Kufi hat and carrying an American flag in his shirt pocket. "We are one with members of faith," his voice echoed through the half-filled stadium, "both Jewish, Christian, and others here today and those who are absent. We are believers."

The Yankee stadium prayer service was led by television host Oprah Winfrey and attended by political figures ranging from former President Bill Clinton to New York Mayor Rudolph Giuliani. Those delivering the prayers and short sermons of encouragement reflected the makeup of the city, including a variety of other religious leaders,

---

[99] Ibid., 35.
[100] Ibid., 44.
[101] Translated: "I believe, and I declare that there is no God except the One God."

such as rabbis, Catholic and Eastern Orthodox priests and Protestant ministers.

Following a rousing message by Rev. Dr. Calvin Butts of the Abyssinian Baptist Church, LCMS Atlantic District president Rev. David Benke took the stage: "Oh, we're stronger now than we were an hour ago," he told the crowd. "And you know, my sisters and brothers, we're not nearly as strong as we're going to be. And the strength we have is the power of love. And the power of love you have received is from God, for God is love. So take the hand of one next to you now and join me in prayer on this 'field of dreams' turned into God's house of prayer."[102]

As Benke prayed, television cameras panned across audience members reaching across stadium seats to hold each other's hands. On the podium, Rabbi Marc Gellman joined hands with Imam Pasha and the two bowed their heads.

"O Lord our God, we're leaning on You today," he prayed, "You are our Tower of Strength, and we're leaning on You. You are our Mighty Fortress, our God who is a Rock; in You do we stand. Those of us who bear the name of Christ know that You stood so tall when You stooped down to send a Son through death and life to bring us back together, and we lean on You today."

"O Tower of Strength, open innocent and victimized hearts to the sacrifice of the Innocent One; pour Your consolation upon the traumatized, especially our children," he continued, "O Heavenly Father, un-bind, un-fear, un-scorch, un-sear our souls; renew us in Your free Spirit. We're leaning on You, our Tower of Strength. We find our refuge in the shadow of Your shelter. Lead us from this place--strong--to bring forth the power of Your love, wherever we are. In the precious name of Jesus, amen."

---

[102] "New York City Prayer Service," C-SPAN, 23 September 2001.

The audience applauded as Benke finished, and as Winfrey took the podium to conduct the final segments of the prayer service. Benke's prayer for strength and safety was a subdued transition into the final portion of the gathering. However, his participation set off a firestorm in the Lutheran Church-Missouri Synod, leading to heresy charges against the Brooklyn pastor and nearly toppling the head of the denomination.

For his participation in the service with ministers of other faiths and denominations, Benke was suspended from his clerical duties, and charged with "unionism" and "syncretism." The LCMS defined the terms in the following manner: "Syncretism and unionism are different in that syncretism deals with the blending in worship of Christians with pagan religions, or non-Christians. Unionism deals with the bringing together for worship various Christian groups/denominations which officially preach and teach different and even opposing doctrines."[103] In all, 21 LCMS pastors and three congregations complained of Benke's role in the Yankee Stadium service.

Prior to joining the roster of ministers at the prayer service, Benke received permission from the denomination's president, Rev. Gerald Kieschnick, who reportedly considered it an "innocent public event." However, a rift in the LCMS leadership occurred when Rev. Wallace Shulz, the denomination's second vice president, suspended Benke from the clergy rolls. In turn, Wallace was suspended from being main speaker on the radio program "The Lutheran Hour. The radio ministry's board considered Wallace's action a conflict of interest and a violation of their code of ethics.[104]

Rev. Daniel Preus, whose father led the 1973 faculty walkout at Concordia Seminary, was now first vice president of the denomination, Preus helped lead the charge among those condemning Benke's participation. "I cannot come to any conclusion except that his participation was wrong," he wrote to a fellow LCMS minister. "The

---

[103] Wallace Schulz, "Schulz Report," 3.

[104] Jim Suhr, "Lutherans Divided," Associated Press, 2 August 2002.

more I learn about the events, the more I am convinced that it was a unionistic and syncretistic service for it not only involved Christians of differing beliefs in a common service but even brought pagans and Christians together in prayer as though all were praying to the same god or as though prayers to false gods are as valid and effective as those to the only true God, the Triune God."[105]

The Benke controversy not only threatened the status of the minister who prayed at Yankee Stadium, but also the status of denomination's president. Kieschnick was a minister and active leader in the LCMS for more than two decades. His presidency of the denomination began on September 8, 2001 – almost literally on the eve of the attacks. (Kieschnick was installed as the 12th president by a slim vote of 50.8 percent.) President Kieschnick stood as Benke's top defender in his dispute between the LCMS vice presidents, as well as the faculty of Concordia seminary and a few congregations in the 2.6 million-member denomination.

Kieschnick's opinion going into office was that the denomination should improve its relationship with the Evangelical Lutheran Church of America. However, the delegates in the denomination's July 2001 convention rejected this idea, adopting the statement, "We cannot consider [the ELCA] to be an orthodox Lutheran church body."[106]

After the news of the Yankee stadium event swept through the denomination, Kieschnick himself was charged with unionism and syncretism. Two pastors sought to have him expelled for his approval of Benke's participation in the service and for his own participation with ELCA members at a September 19, 2001 event at Holy Trinity

---

[105] Daniel Preus, "Letter to Pastor Steve Flo," 3 October 2001.

[106] "Briefs: North America," *Christianity Today*, July 2001.

Lutheran Church in Manhattan.[107] LCMS delegates voided the charges against Kieschnick before the year was out.[108]

In May 2003, Benke was reinstated to his position as president of the LCMS Atlantic district and was able to return to his Brooklyn pulpit. A panel investigating the charges concluded: "Rev. Benke's prayer, even though criticized by many, was Christian."[109] The embattled minister said he spent the period out of the pulpit running a Lutheran social services organization that provides help for the homeless, foster care, and other services.[110]

During the July 2004 LCMS convention, delegates cast their votes on whether Kieschnick should be re-elected as the conservative denomination's president. When the voting was over and the ballots counted, Kieschnick held up a sign given to him by his wife, which said "It's a Wonderful Life." He had been re-elected by a 52.8 percent margin. Vice President Daniel Preus, who helped lead the movement to oust Kieschnick and banish Benke from the clergy rolls was voted out of office during the same convention.[111]

Fuller Seminary: Foundations for Peacemaking

In 2003, the nondenominational evangelical Fuller Seminary engaged in a "Conflict Transformation" project funded by a $993,500 grant through the Department of Justice. The funding was among a series of assistance grants provided by the Justice Department, with

---

[107] Bill Broadway, "The Limits of Religious Unity," *Washington Post*, 21 November 2001, B09.

[108] "Ruling Voids Charges Against Kieschnick," *LCMSNews - No. 97*, 11 December 2001.

[109] Jim Suhr, "Pastor Cleared After Praying With 'Pagans,'" *Associated Press*, 13 May 2003.

[110] Alan Cooperman, "Minister's Suspension Over 9-11 Service Lifted," *Washington Post*, 13 May 2003, A07.

[111] "Lutheran President Re-Elected," *Associated Press*, 12 July 2004.

similar amounts going to organizations and communities in California running anti-gang and crime prevention programs.[112]

The objective of the Fuller project is to create a paradigm for constructive dialogue between the evangelical and Muslim communities. Among those goals, as stated in the project's outline, are to extend evangelical efforts in "just peacemaking theory" (in contrast to just war theory, and distinct from theories that oppose any use of force) to influence peacemaking practices in the Muslim community.[113] Project leaders hoped to promote just peacemaking by working with Muslims to address issues that lead to conflict. Among the responses to conflict they are suggesting are working with cooperative institutions such as the United Nations as well as fostering "just and sustainable" economic development. The project also hopes to provide a forum to discuss democracy, religious liberty and the use of "partnership conflict resolution" in resolving issues that sometimes lead to violence.[114]

One of the first products of the Fuller grant was a draft of a Code of Ethics for dialogue between Muslims, as represented by the Islamic Center of Southern California, and evangelical Christians, as represented by Fuller Seminary. The goal of the code was to increase understanding between the two groups as well as open channels of communication and cooperation.

The code for the practice of dialogue consisted of seven, mostly non-controversial, points:

1. An Ethic of Mutual Care for The Other as a Full and Equal partner in Conversation, Rights and Practice.

2. An Ethic of Truthfulness.

---

[112] *Fiscal Year 2003 Bureau of Justice Earmarks*, Department of Justice, 17 June 2003, 2.

[113] *Conflict Transformation Grant: Creating Collaboration and Reducing Conflict in Muslim-Christian Relationships*, Fuller Theological Seminary.

[114] Glen Stassen, "New Paradigm: Just Peacemaking Theory."

3. An Ethic of Commitment to Understand the Other, as Accurately as Possible.

4. An Ethic of learning from Each Other and Sharing knowledge and Values.

5. An Ethic of Caring for the Neighbor

6. An Ethic of Respect for Each Other's Integrity and Dignity

7. An Ethic of Continuing Commitment to be Constructive, to be Open to Complexity and Unafraid of Ambiguity.[115]

The more controversial portion of the code was a "declaration" by both Muslims and evangelicals. Some evangelical leaders, such as John Revell of the Southern Baptist Executive Committee, said the affirmation in the code that Christians and Muslims worship the same God is a "radical departure, not only from the Evangelical tradition but also the tenets of orthodoxy."[116]

Of particular concern for many evangelical leaders, including Revell, was the agreement for both sides to not attempt conversion of the other during the project. Some evangelicals saw no basis for theological or social discussion between adherents of the two religions, as the Fuller project prescribed. Among the critics was R. Albert Mohler Jr., President of the Southern Baptist Theological Seminary. "The more we know about Christianity and Islam," Mohler said, "the more we see there is a basic incompatibility. The essential ground of conflict and controversy cannot be removed."[117]

---

[116] Teresa Watanabe, "Seminary is Reaching Out to Muslims," *Los Angeles Times*, 6 December 2003, B1.

[117] Ted Olsen, "Weblog: Fuller Seminary to Create Interfaith Code of Ethics," *ChristianityToday.com*, 8 December 2003.

The code differs from the one produced by the Institute for Religion and Democracy in May 2003 in that the IRD code focuses much more on presenting a full view of Christianity to Muslims without "over-simplifying" the differences and commonalities between the two religions. While the Fuller code promotes understanding, and sets the stage for cooperative efforts on a variety of fronts, evangelism remains at the heart of the IRD document. For example, the IRD code explicitly states that the goal of Muslim-Christian dialogue is to "Give testimony to the Gospel of Jesus Christ, because it is our duty to do so. Ultimately, Christ himself is the greatest blessing that we could offer to our Muslim interlocutors."[118]

With the code of ethics for dialogue in place, Fuller faculty reached out in a number of ways to engage in conversation and other projects with Muslims in southern California and around the United States. One of the primary sources of dialogue and cooperation is the Islamic Shura Council of Southern California. The former head of the council, Yahia Abdul Rahman, remarked on his work with members of Fuller faculty on the project: "We are changing the course away from accusations and poisoning the well of relations to what can develop into a project in the service of God."[119]

However, some Muslims displayed skepticism toward the Fuller project, and its funding provided by the Justice Department. Aslam Abdullah, editor-in-chief of *Minaret* magazine called the project "a big scandal."[120] "It's mostly cosmetics," Abdullah told a reporter for *Christian Century* magazine. "Muslims in southern California have had dialogues at the leadership level the last several decades, yet the

---

[119] John Dart, "U.S. Funds Evangelical – Muslim Project," Christian Century. 27 December 2003.

[120] Bettye Wells Miller, "Shared Religion Viewed as a Vital Tool for Peace," *The Press-Enterprise*, 18 February 2004.

accusations and counteraccusations from both sides by ordinary people have not subsided."[121]

However, Fuller professor Glen Stassen said he and others have spoken to Abdullah since the early days of the project and that most Muslim skeptics have softened their criticism.[122] As for Abdullah, he has since participated in aspects of the program, including a November 20, 2003 event where he discussed similarities between Islam, Christianity and Judaism during an event held at Fuller focusing on the Muslim celebration of Ramadan.[123]

Christianity Today's Internet editor, Ted Olsen, also displayed skepticism in December 2003 about the Fuller project, calling it a "been there, done that" response to rhetoric by Falwell, Graham and others.[124] However, Olsen's senior editors trumped his response in a print issue of the magazine by praising the Fuller project.

An editorial in the January 2004 issue of the magazine pointed out "the faculty members involved had agreed not to proselytize *in the context of these peacemaking discussions* [emphasis theirs]," that the commitment to evangelism remained a part of the Christian participants' identity, and that "Fuller faculty involved in the project have evangelized Muslims both in North America and abroad."[125]

The editorial argued for the appropriateness of putting conversion on hold in certain situations in order to accomplish common goals with Muslims. The key illustration of this was recalled in a conversation between Franklin Graham and President Omar al-Bashir during Graham's visit to Sudan in December 2003 to discuss the country's ongoing civil war. Al-Bashir reportedly told Graham, ""I want freedom

---

[121] Ibid.

[122] Stassen interview.

[123] Press Release, "Muslim Public Affairs Representatives to Speak at Fuller," Fuller Theological Seminary, undated.

[124] Olsen, "Weblog: Fuller Seminary."

[125] "Muslims at Home in America," *Christianity Today*, February 2004, 27.

of religion because I would like to convert you. We will try to make you a Muslim." Graham responded, ""I would like to come back to Khartoum and preach, because I would like to convert you."

The editors argued that dialogue to end political strife was a reasonable instance in which to "defer" efforts to convert, saying "We face a pivotal moment in history when we can help Muslims redefine their place in a modern world. Seize the day."[126]

One of Fuller project's leaders, J. Dudley Woodberry, defended the use of language calling for the recognition of a common God between Muslims and Christians, and the effort to work cooperatively with those in the Muslim community: "The more we can work for common ground, the more chance we have of working through our differences and areas of conflict,"[127]

Speaking specifically to the theological debate over a common deity between Muslims and Christians, Woodberry points out the many evangelicals do not have the same question regarding Judaism:

> The differences are essentially the same differences we have with contemporary Jews who do not follow Jesus. Yet most Christians would say that Jews worship the same God, even though they do not understand or accept his revelation in Jesus Christ. As one who is studying Muslim conversions to Christ and is privileged to teach in a school whose former students are probably involved in leading more Muslims to faith in Christ than those of any other school, a majority of the converts that I have seen understand their conversion as bringing them into a personal relationship to the One God whom they knew less completely and misunderstood before.[128]

---

[126] Ibid.

[127] Miller, "Shared Religion."

[128] Hans Cornelder, "More On Fuller's Interfaith Conflict Resolution Effort," 13 December 2003.

As the project unfolded, the Justice Department money was used to bring in Muslim, Christian and secular scholars from around the United States to Fuller for consultations, travel grants for Ph.D. students, as well as salaries for personnel working on the program. Among the goals of the consultations and research funded by the project were two books slated for production, one on "Muslim-Christian Conflict Reduction and Transformation," and another on "Practices of Just Peacemaking in Muslim Tradition and the Quran."[129]

The Boundaries of Discourse

These three cases highlight disputes within evangelicalism over what sociologists Benford and Snow, among others, have labeled boundary and adversarial framing. Adversarial framing tends to find a source of blame for an adverse situation (such as terrorism or threats to security).[130] On the evangelical "family farm" where the movement's ideologies are grown, each of these members viewed the Christian response to Sept. 11th as a problem in need of a solution to protect their own identity and security. However, each defined the problem and the solution differently, thus creating a range of environments for productive evangelical-Muslim discourse.

For example, among many leaders and activists in the Southern Baptist Convention, the cause of September 11th and the outpouring of conflict between the Muslim world and the West are rooted in Islam itself. SBC literature and statements by prominent figures in the denomination have painted Islam as not only uniform in its theology, but interwoven with calls to violence (i.e. Emir and Ergun Caner's writings, and their influence on leaders such as Jerry Vines.)[131]

---

129 *Conflict Transformation Grant.*

130 Benford and Snow, "Frame Processes and Social Movements," 616.

131 Emir Caner and Ergun Caner, "The Doctrine of Jihad in the Islamic Hadith."

The Southern Baptist Convention's response was to rearticulate the differences between Christianity and Islam, highlight passages in the Quran and Sunnah that call for violence against the "infidel," and call for increased missionary efforts to present the Gospel as an alternative to Islam. The ground here remained thorny for Muslim-Christian dialogue, choking out efforts to form a positive mode of discourse between Christians and Muslims except in narrowly defined theological debates.

The denomination's approach to the "Islamic threat" did not go unchallenged. Members of the extended evangelical family, including the NAE and some Baptists outside the SBC rebuked Vines and Falwell for rhetoric that they saw as damaging to Muslim-Christian relations. However, the SBC did not turn away from their assessment of the threat.

Within the Lutheran Church-Missouri Synod, the key "threat" continued to revolve around the denomination's potential departure from Lutheran orthodoxy. In the Benke case, the leadership was split over whether the Brooklyn minister crossed boundaries meant to protect the purity of the denomination when he prayed at an interfaith service at Yankee Stadium. The proper response to this threat was seen by a number of congregations, ministers and the denomination's vice presidents as the removal from leadership of those who participated in, and approved of, participation in interfaith events, as seen in the heresy charges against Benke and Kieschnick.[132]

In this case, the dispute over the solution to the problem came within the denomination itself. Though the denomination has a long history of protectionism toward its doctrine and practice, LCMS delegates eventually restored Benke to his previous post, and Kieschnick was re-elected to the denomination's presidency by an even wider margin than he was initially voted into office. In this case, the denomination took a historic step beyond previous ideological boundaries by allowing a limited form of participation for its ministers

[132] "Schulz Report."

outside of its own denomination. Though the LCMS retains strict rules against full communion with other Christian churches, and the theological barrier remains high toward other religions, the seeds of dialogue may find root among certain LCMS ministers who call for Christians to remain engaged with a religiously pluralistic world without violating their own orthodoxy.[133]

For Fuller seminary, blame for hatred and violence was not placed on a religious group or violation of a set of tenets, but on ignorance and behaviors among Christians and Muslims that distance the two religious communities from each other. Their solution was to reach out to the Muslim community and engage in a well-funded effort to increase understanding and reduce conflict. Just as the SBC was criticized by for their assessment of the threat and solution, some in the extended evangelical family criticized Fuller for deferring efforts to convert and engaging in a more comprehensive plan of cultural and theological conversation. However, the project eventually received praise from many Christian and Muslim leaders, and from the evangelical media.[134]

In the case of Fuller seminary, the threat was seen as the environment of hostility itself. Though some faculty expressed concerns about remaining true to evangelical identity, an effort was made to enrich the soil so that seeds of dialogue and understanding could thrive, and the tares of conflict would wither. Each response showed the diversity of ideology that exists within the bounds of evangelicalism, and the disputes among its members that strain the cohesiveness of the movement itself.

---

[133] Don Matzat, "The Christian in a Culture of Religious Pluralism."
[134] "Muslims at Home in America," *Christianity Today.*

WALTER R. RATLIFF

3

POLITICS, RELIGION AND THE END TIMES

Dispensationalist eschatology looms large on the minds of many, but not all, evangelicals. The immense popularity of books such as Hal Lindsay's *Late Great Planet Earth* in the 1970's, Edgar Whisenant's *88 Reasons The Rapture Could Be in 1988*, and the tremendously popular *Left Behind* series by Tim LaHaye and Jerry Jenkins from the mid-1990's onward, show a continuity of interest in the End Times, and a desire to relate current events to biblical prophecies.

These books each present the threat of a secular, liberal world order as the chief catalyst for the final events leading to the return of Christ. In Lindsay's book and the *Left Behind* series, the Antichrist arises out of secular institutions such as a European Union and the United Nations, with the rebirth of the state of Israel playing a prominent role. Whether the Antichrist emerged from the Soviet Union, the European Union, or the United Nations, the institutions that were seen as embodying the threat were all modern, secular institutions. This emphasis on secular European institutions largely replaced earlier fundamentalist suspicions about the Roman Catholic Church fostering the Antichrist.

It is no surprise that the events of September 11th also had an impact on how some evangelicals see the Last Days playing out. A prime example of how discourse has changed toward Muslims after the Sept. 11 attacks is in a series of sermons delivered by Lon Solomon at McLean Bible Church. McLean is an evangelical non-denominational mega-church in the suburbs of Washington, DC that uses a "seeker-sensitive model," often incorporating movie clips, contemporary music, and dynamic translations of the Bible into the services in an effort to appeal to those outside the evangelical subculture. Solomon himself comes from a Jewish background. He converted to Christianity in 1971, earned a master's degree and did doctoral work at Johns Hopkins University in Near Eastern Studies. He also taught Hebrew and Old Testament courses at Capital Bible Seminary.[135]

In a sermon on January 7, 2002 delivered to the church's young adult Frontline church service, attended weekly by about 2,500 single adults from the Washington, DC area, Solomon dismissed previous speculation from fundamentalist and evangelical teachers about the origins of the Antichrist:

> You may have heard the Antichrist is going to come from Europe. You may have heard the Antichrist is going to come from China. You may have heard the Antichrist is going to come from Russia. I'm here to tell you that Babylon in the Bible means Babylon. And Russia isn't mentioned in connection with the Antichrist. Europe isn't mentioned. Rome isn't mentioned. China isn't mentioned. America isn't mentioned. Babylon is mentioned time after time, and that's

---

[135] *Records of the Department of Near Eastern Studies,* Johns Hopkins University. Lon Solomon is listed as a student in the department from 1976-1985.

where I believe it's got to happen. God, you, know, if he meant Rome he would have said Rome.[136]

Solomon emphasized in the sermon that he was not labeling Saddam Hussein or Osama bin Laden as the Antichrist, nor was he ruling them out. However, he did put Islam squarely in the path of eschatological events:

> If we are correct, it means that Islam, or some offshoot of Islam is going to be the religious system of the Antichrist and his kingdom. And you know folks, we have seen in recent years the ability of Islam to be molded into hero worship by people who distort it. We've seen, we've all got the mental images of the Ayatollah Khomeini in Iran, Saddam Hussein in Iraq, of Muammar Qaddafi in Libya, of Osama bin Laden. And as the end of the age approaches, if we are correct, we should see all the major Islamic nations of the Middle East pulling together to follow some mesmerizing leader who's ruling from Babylon in the modern country of Iraq.[137]

Solomon concluded his sermon by encouraging the audience members to be "diligent" in efforts to evangelize. He also outlines a scenario in which, after believers are raptured at the beginning of the Tribulation, the Antichrist emerges, and 144,000 Jews turn to Christianity and become "kosher Billy Grahams" preaching the gospel.[138] Though Islam is portrayed as the incubator of the Antichrist, Solomon stopped short of telling Christians to approach Muslims as adversaries."[139]

This sermon stands in contrast to a message on Islam that Solomon delivered eleven years before. During the February 1991

---

[136] Lon Solomon, "Will the Real Antichrist Please Stand Up?" McLean Bible Church, 7 January 2002.

[137] Ibid.

[138] Ibid.

[139] Juergensmeyer, *Terror in the Mind of God.*

sermon, he outlined the religion's basic beliefs, and disputed them with the teachings of Christianity. What was missing in the sermon, delivered on the heels of the Persian Gulf War, was the eschatological connection between Islam and the Antichrist, and anything but a theological opposition to Islam.[140]

When it comes to evangelical-Muslim relations, McLean Bible Church holds an interesting position in the nation's capital region. Although the pulpit rhetoric from the naturally takes an oppositional stance to Islam, there is a level of openness among important members of the congregation with regard to relationships with Muslims.

Although McLean Bible Church is not officially involved with interfaith dialogue with Muslims, members of the congregation come from many sectors of Washington's political and public community. For example, Dr. Jennifer Bryson is a former member of McLean Bible Church who now leads the Islam and Civil Society project at the Witherspoon Institute in Princeton New Jersey.

At a 2009 panel dealing with the concept of respect between evangelicals and Muslims, Bryson told of her experience with those outside the church:

> Professionally, I am in Arabic and Islamic studies. I would meet people and we would have these great discussions about what is happening with Islam in the world and my work. And then they would find out I went to McLean Bible Church. And they would say, oh "those people," and go on with stereotypes. And I would ask them, how many people have you met that go to McLean Bible Church? How much time have you spent as a fly on the wall at a dinner party with people who go to McLean Bible Church, or have really honest internal disagreements and differences, and are really trying to work through their faith lives together? This is where if we can look at "respect" as respecting human beings, as respecting Muslims as respecting

---

[140] Solomon, "Islam," McLean Bible Church, 2 February 1991.

Christians, we can also recognize that within each faith community there is not going to be a monolith. This type of respect also encourages us to do more listening when we encounter the "Other."[141]

At the same panel, Imam Mohammed Magid of Northern Virginia's largest Mosque, the ADAMS Center, complimented McLean Bible Church:

> Evangelicals and Muslims in America have a lot to work with, and I am glad to be having this conversation here. Many Muslims have felt that the attacks on the prophet, the attacks on Muhammad (peace be upon him), represents all evangelical groups, because some of them have not been at McLean Bible Church – which is around the corner from me by the way, and they do a great job with social service and social justice. Therefore there is a lot of mistrust and misunderstanding taking place here.[142]

Former Congressman and UN Ambassador Mark Siljander is another member of McLean Bible Church that has recently made a career of reaching across religious lines to Muslims. Siljander's book, *A Deadly Misunderstanding: A Congressman's Quest to Bridge the Muslim-Christian Divide*, goes further than most evangelical literature in connecting theologically-conservative theology with the Muslim understanding of Jesus and sacred scriptures. Siljander's current work is an about-face from his earlier stances against Muslims when he was a member if the United States House of Representatives. During the 1980s, Siljander was the epitome of an arch-conservative Republican member of Congress, championing staunch opposition to abortion rights and promoting pro-Israel foreign policy. As a freshman congressman, Siljander sent an angry letter to the emcee of the

---

[141] Global Leadership Forum: "Evangelicals and Muslims: Conversations on Respect, Reconciliation and Religious Freedom," Institute for Global Engagement and the Prince Alwaleed bin Talal Center for the Muslim-Christian Understanding, Georgetown University, 17 June 2009.
[142] Ibid.

National Prayer Breakfast after he heard an imam reading from the Quran. Rep. Siljander questioned the organizers choice, demanding "How can you read the book of the devil at a prayer breakfast?"[143]

Decades later, Siljander's attitude toward Muslims and the Quran has changed dramatically. His book chronicles his reassessment of the Muslim world and the religion of Islam that he undertook after leaving public office. The book recounts his personal experiences with Muslim religious leaders, and compares the similarities between Jesus as portrayed in the Quran with Jesus as he is described in the Aramaic New Testament (the *lingua franca* of first-century Palestine).

In an interview with a *Read the Spirit* website blogger, Siljander recalls his days in Congress ("I was an arrogant young punk politician."), and his current work on Islam and Christianity. The interviewer also brings up the subject of McLean Bible Church:

David: What fascinates me about your work is that you remain a devout Christian. You attend a conservative, evangelical church in McLean, Virginia. And yet you argue passionately — and work in daring ways — to push Christians toward friendly, constructive dialogue rather than hateful confrontation. That's amazing.

Mark: I'm not an apologist for the Quran or for Islam. I'm an apologist for Jesus. I'm just trying to move people from this very negative point of view of Islam. It's in the title of my book. The view of Islam by so many Christians is really just a big mishmash of "Deadly Misunderstanding." The vast majority of Muslims — like the vast majority of Christians — want to lead peaceful lives. To force Muslims into a corner where there's nowhere left to turn is a deadly mistake. That gives power to militants who are talking about killing people. I'm not telling people to go become Muslim. I'm a Christian. But there are more than a billion people in the world who we

---

[143] Brian Ervin, "Seeking Common Ground," *Urban Tulsa Weekly*, 28 November 2007.

all ought to know a lot better. Christians ought to know Muslims. By learning about each other, we all can support moderates and endorse a peaceful interpretation of scriptures.[144]

However, other old-guard influentials within the evangelical community continue to see American Muslims as a threat to traditional American values and institutions. The widely-syndicated columnist Cal Thomas stated his position clearly: "Government officials warn that America remains in danger from Al Qaeda and other terrorist operatives who wish to destroy us. This is not a one-front war, because we also face dangers from within our democratic institutions."[145]

Thomas went on to cite the political objectives of the Council on American-Islamic Relations as raising the profile of Islam and Muslims in the American public square, alongside criticism from Daniel Pipes that CAIR is "consistently defending militant Islamic groups and dictators, while 'denouncing' terrorist acts." He also cites census figures from Canada showing the rapid rise in the country's Muslim population. He wrote that the consequences for Muslim political participation are dire for American society and foreign policy:

> You don't have to be paranoid to fear where this can lead in Canada and in the United States -where immigration and births are dramatically increasing the Muslim population. Vote-hungry politicians might easily bow to the political objectives of Muslim voters, many of whom have agendas outside this country and, in fact, outside this world. When Muslims gain political power, the historical and contemporary record is not encouraging for people who hold democratic values and are of the "Judeo-Christian" persuasion. If politicians succumb to pressure from Muslim activist groups and equate Islam with the religious and political heritage of this country, we will know that an important beachhead has been attained by our enemies.

[144]David Crumm, "Conversation With Mark Siljander," Read the Spirit Blog.
[145] Cal Thomas, "The Threat Among Us," *Baltimore Sun*, 21 May 2003, 19A.

From their behavior in other parts of the world, one can safely predict they will use this beachhead to advance their cause.[146]

These and other examples illustrate how some members of the evangelical family view Muslims, whether in the form of their American Muslim neighbors or the religion of Islam itself, as a threat that must be guarded against or phenomena that must be respected and engaged. This rhetoric shows how competing narratives are emerging within the evangelical community, creating a growing rift between those who frame Muslims as adversaries and those who wish for positive engagement.

Some evangelicals have taken engagement a step further, by presenting the Gospel as something that can be spread while building solid friendships that go beyond efforts where the goal is simply conversion. Jamie Winship is a missionary and freelance writer that has worked in Indonesia, Iraq and among Muslims in the United States. On June 28, 2003 Winship delivered a one-day presentation on Islam at Reston Bible Church in northern Virginia. During the three-hour talk, Winship argued that evangelism needs to be contextualized by emphasizing the commonalities between the two faiths. Standing before an overhead projector displaying a list of theological assertions Winship said:

> I love to go into a church, write these statements down and say, 'Where do you find that.' And of course they'll say it's in the Bible, it's an evangelical position. Look, Jesus is the Word of God. Jesus is a spirit from God. Jesus was led by the Holy Spirit. Jesus was born of a virgin. Jesus guides people to truth. Jesus is a sign for all people. Jesus is to be obeyed. Jesus is a servant of God and a prophet. Jesus was righteous. Look at the next statement. Muhammad was not righteous. Jesus did miracles. Jesus knows the future. Jesus is the mediator between God and man. Jesus would die for unbelievers. Jesus resurrected from the dead. Jesus ascended into heaven after his

---

[146] Ibid.

death and resurrection. Jesus is the author of creation. Jesus is coming again. All from the Quran – every single one of those statements... if this is the case, can't you just now see a way to talk to your Muslim friends?[147]

Winship, who referred several times to his membership in a Southern Baptist church, argued before the gathering at the non-denominational church that evangelicals often don't realize the cultural baggage and the Christian terminology that   are often mystifying or offensive to Muslims. In order to bring the audience around to a positive view of Muslims, he spent a large portion of the presentation on portraying Arabs and Muslims as spiritually connected to Jews and Christians through common roots reaching back to Abraham, Hagar and Sarah.

Among the more controversial approaches Winship took in his effort to proselytize Muslims was his attempt to use the Quran as the authority in an effort to prove the Bible, particularly the Old Testament, has not been corrupted. Winship is unapologetic about his wish to convert his Muslim friends. He argues that seeing Muslims as enemies hurts one of the basic tenets of evangelicalism: "Muslims, the sons and daughters of Ishmael, are a people of promise from God (Genesis 16, 21). Often we view them as adversaries and are afraid to share Christ with them. Yet we know God will only rejoice in His holy temple when every tribe, tongue, and people have heard the gospel."[148]

Winship relates the story of his involvement with Azam Shahadeh, a Palestinian imam living in his neighborhood. Winship cultivated a friendship with Azam that included arguing theological differences between Islam and Christianity, but also standing beside him, his family and members of the mosque in a number of situations that were difficult for the traditional Muslims living in the United States.

---

[147] Jamie Winship, "Christianity and Islam," Reston Bible Church, 28 June 2003.

[148] Winship, "Faith, Hope, Love, Azam," *Discipleship Journal*, September-October 2003.

This included Winship bringing his family to sit with the Shahadeh family during football games where Azam's son was playing. Azam and his wife were often left sitting alone because of their dress and appearance (as well as Fahima Shahadeh's ululating during exciting moments in the game). Winship's engagement also included a presentation on behalf of the local mosque before the city council when zoning laws made it difficult for local Muslims to observe traditional burial practices. In turn, Azam has attended certain special services at Winship's church, and has invited his Christian friend to speak on numerous occasions in the mosque. Azam has not converted to Christianity, but Winship describes a deep level of friendship and respect between them, their families and the Muslims and Christian communities in their North Carolina town.[149]

Political Fault Lines

During the 2004 presidential election, the majorities of Muslims and evangelicals found themselves on opposite sides of the fence when it comes to their party affiliation and choice for president.[150] In a major poll by Georgetown University's Project MAPS and Zogby International, Muslims were observed as shifting toward the Democratic Party during the Bush administration, disagreeing strongly with the administration's foreign policy in the Middle East (notably the support of Israel as well as the war in Iraq) and domestic policies they view as leading to civil rights violations.[151] Comparing the MAPS poll with recent polls of evangelicals helps paint a picture of how the Muslim and evangelical communities stand in relation to each other in the public square.

---

[149] Ibid.
[150] *Shifting Political Winds & Fallout from 9/11, Afghanistan, and Iraq*, Project MAPS, Zogby International, October 2004.
[151] Ibid. 32-37.

The MAPS survey showed Muslims supporting Sen. John Kerry's bid for the White House by a margin of 76 percent. On the other hand, a Barna poll released in June 2004 characterized evangelicals as a crucial group for Bush, supporting his re-election by 86 percent.[152]

Despite the divergent political orientations, polls suggested some common sympathies between evangelicals and American Muslims on certain hot political topics. For example, a Pew Research Center poll shows 84 percent of evangelicals oppose gay marriage.[153] The Project MAPS poll shows similar opposition from Muslims at 79 percent.[154] The two polls also show identical opposition to physician-assisted suicide between the two communities by a margin of 61-31 percent.[155] The Project MAPS poll also showed a majority of American Muslims support vouchers for parents who want to send their children to religious schools, government funding for religious institutions providing social services, and even the display of the Ten Commandments in public schools – all key domestic issues for the evangelical community.[156]

However, when it comes to support for government assistance to the poor, government involvement to end racial discrimination, and universal health care, these issues are all strongly supported by Muslims, and have weaker support among white evangelicals.

Although an atmosphere of cooperation with Muslims is not being cultivated by a large segment of the evangelical family, there are those who are forging the cultural tools to engage Muslims on a variety of levels. However, there are certain obstacles that this segment of evangelicals may have a difficult time overcoming. These obstacles are mirrored in the mix of common causes and divergent agendas between

[152] "Tight Presidential Race Influenced by People's Faith," The Barna Group, 7 June 2004.

[153] *Contention and Consensus*, Pew Research Center, 24 July 2003, 17.

[154] Project MAPS, 38.

[155] Ibid., 20.

[156] Ibid.

African-American and white evangelicals painted by Michael Emerson and Christian Smith in the book *Divided by Faith*.

Emerson and Smith document how evangelicals, including Southern Baptists and groups such as Promise Keepers, have attempted to overcome racial boundaries that separate them from African-Americans who hold similar theological views. They say white evangelicals "want to see an end to race problems because both their Christian faith and their faith in the American creed call for it." However, the authors say that the solutions proposed by evangelicals (building cross-race relationships, opposing individual cases of discrimination, etc.) do not address the systemic inequalities within American society and the evangelical subculture.[157]

Theological and cultural attributes of evangelicalism often pass over institutional problems that require solutions that go beyond individual responses. evangelicals are often unwilling to get behind political issues important to their black counterparts.[158] Those issues of concern to other American minorities often coincide with the concerns of American Muslims, including policies on civil rights and government assistance to the poor, which are usually not part of the evangelical community's political repertoire.

That being the case, those evangelicals seeking engagement with Muslims face significant challenges. First, although approaching Muslims with openness and positive dialogue is advocated by a number of important leaders and institutions within evangelicalism, polls show a growing suspicion within the movement toward Islam and Muslims.[159] evangelicals ranging from the Fuller faculty to Jamie Winship will likely continue to battle against a competing view within their movement that portrays Islam as "evil and wicked," and Muslims as theological adversaries.

---

[157] Emerson and Smith, 130.

[158] Ibid., 170.

[159] "Evangelical Views of Islam."

Second, even though Muslims and evangelical Christians stand on the same side of a range of social political issues, the two groups increasingly are allied with parties on the opposite side of the aisle. Up to and following the re-election of George Bush, evangelicals enjoyed significant power and influence in the Republican party. Muslims are increasingly regard the Democratic party as looking out for their best interests.

Third, the broad evangelical support for Israel remains a crucial issue and a stumbling block on the path toward engagement with Muslims. Fuller Seminary's Dudley Woodberry summed up the issue by saying that "pro-Zionist views" among evangelicals generate the same level of offense to Muslims as negative remarks about Islam.[160]

However, there are signs that Muslims and Arabs in the United States and abroad recognize the diversity of the evangelical movement, and the potential for positive engagement. James Zogby, president of the Arab American Institute, views right wing evangelical activists as a subset of the broader movement:

> Listen, there are evangelicals and there are evangelicals.
> Actually, I founded the Palestine Human Rights Campaign and
> we had a lot of evangelical Christians who supported
> Palestinian human rights. I believe that there is a born-again
> movement that has a right wing tilt - the Christian Coalition.
> That is a problem, not just for Arab-Americans and Muslims,
> but it's a problem for many constituent groups in America.[161]

Zogby also said, "being born-again is not antithetical" to listening and working with Arabs and Muslims. In the effort to repair the movement's image abroad, the National Association of Evangelicals has been working to build relationships with governments in the Muslim world. In April 2004, the National Association of Evangelicals announced that had reached an agreement with the

---

[160] Woodberry interview.

[161] James Zogby, interview by author, 26 July 2004.

Kingdom of Morocco to begin a "wide-ranging dialogue with evangelicals on religious and cultural issues." The NAE cited a Pew poll in their announcement that observed 73 percent of Moroccans had "unfavorable attitudes" toward Christians, which the NAE participants hoped to improve.[162] The NAE and Moroccan government also scheduled a "Friendship Fest" in Marrakech in May 2005 featuring contemporary Christian music alongside contemporary and traditional Moroccan music, as well as "respectful dialogues" designed to "combat terrorism by confronting stereotypes on both sides that lead to extremist rhetoric."[163]

Leaders such as Rev. Richard Cizik, the NAE's former Vice President of Governmental Affairs, are also seeking to observe the relationship between Islam and society in the country, and "investigate whether this particularly moderate form of Islam can serve as an antidote to Wahhabism and other forms of religion-based extremism." Rev. Rob Schenck, of the National Clergy Council said the engagement by the Moroccan government and evangelicals "represents an exceptional opportunity for us to learn more about a face of Islam we had never experienced, a loving, respectful approach to others."[164]

The NAE also began expanding its political advocacy beyond that of persecuted Christians abroad by taking on issues that would help build credibility among Muslims. A prime example is the NAE's interest in urging the Bush administration to "take decisive action – including exploration of all intervention strategies – to prevent further slaughter and death" in Sudan's Darfur region. In adopting this cause, the NAE's former president, Ted Haggard, said in 2004, "We view this

---

[162] "Evangelical Christians Strike Breakthrough Accord With Moroccan Government," National Association of Evangelicals, 8 April 2004.

[163] "Friendship Fest Morocco 2005," National Association of Evangelicals, undated.

[164] "Evangelical Christians Strike Breakthrough Accord."

as an opportunity to reach out to Muslims, in the name of Jesus, and to speak out with one voice."[165]

New Directions

A decade after the Sept. 11th attacks, evangelicals were reconsidering their close association with Republican politics. An important moment in this shift was during the 2008 presidential campaign. Rick Warren, one of the most highly influential evangelicals of the past decade, held a presidential forum in Orange County, Calif. at his church, which is affiliated with the Southern Baptist Convention. The controversial forum at Saddleback Church was seen as an effort by Democrat presidential candidate Barack Obama to reach out to evangelicals.

Warren angered some evangelicals in 2006 and 2007 when Obama and Hillary Clinton had appeared during the Global Summits on AIDS and the Church. Saddleback Church clarified through a press release that they do not endorse the views of each speaker at the conference (particularly those who advocate abortion rights), but "the Summit speakers are affirming and supporting the vital role of the Church in fighting the pandemic of HIV/AIDS."

In the release, the church reiterated its official commitment to the pro-life perspective. However, Warren stated: "To be truly pro-life means far more than opposing abortion. It also means doing everything in our power to keep people alive, so they might respond to the grace of Jesus Christ. Sometimes that means working with people you disagree with. With AIDS killing 8,000 people a day, saving lives is more important to us than political alignment."[166]

---

[165] "Evangelical Leaders Urge President Bush to Take Decisive Action to Prevent Slaughter in Darfur," National Association of Evangelicals, 2 August 2004.
[166] Larry Ross, "Statement by Saddleback Valley Community Church," *Christian Newswire*, 1 September 2001.

Other evangelical leaders have also softened their solidarity with conservative politics and the Republican Party, and embraced a broader view of whom they will work with. This has also translated into some movement in the realm of evangelical-Muslim relations.

Joel C. Rosenberg

Another evangelical leader who has demonstrated this type of shift is author and political strategist Joel C. Rosenberg. He is known for his bestselling *Last Jihad* series of novels and his nonfiction titles *Epicenter* (unrelated to this book) and *Inside the Revolution*. Rosenberg occupies an interesting place in evangelical culture because his influence cuts across political and cultural lines within the movement. Like Hal Lindsay, he has produced nonfiction books and films (*Epicenter* and *Epicenter 2.0*) that attempt to show current events as fulfillments of prophetic scripture, and warn readers that the End Times are near. Like Tim LaHaye and Jerry Jenkins, he has produced popular fiction titles that have sparked the apocalyptic imaginations of readers. He also has worked as a political operative for Republican politicians, including presidential candidate Steve Forbes, as well as Israeli politicians ranging from Natan Sharansky to Benjamin Netanyahu.

Rosenberg's fiction draws from the dispensationalist outline of the fulfillment of prophecy in the Middle East, with Islamic jihadists filling the role that the Catholic Church, the Soviet Union and other perceived enemies of the True Church did in similar apocalyptic storylines. Rosenberg's later fiction, as well as his nonfiction titles, have focused on Iran as a rising nuclear power in the region.

In his *Epicenter* books, Rosenberg outlines his view of world events unfolding according to biblical prophecy. In a later edition of *Epicenter*, Rosenberg says he produced his nonfiction works to help explain the thinking behind his fiction stories, which, he argues, have partially come true. Rosenberg is clear in pointing out that his predictions and stories have sprung from a way of viewing current events through a particular interpretation of scripture: "My intent with *Epicenter* is not to persuade anyone of what is coming or what these events mean. Rather it is to explain how I came to write novels that seem to have come at least partially true; to explain various Bible prophecies that have not been given enough attention in the past; to answer many questions that have flowed from the novels and the prophecies upon which they were based; to update readers on new events that are relevant to the prophecies described herein."[167]

Rosenberg says most analysis of current events in the Middle East fall short because of their secular focus. Rosenberg says the key to his ability to predict events comes through viewing these events through a prophetic view of scripture: "While it is fashionable in our times to analyze world events merely by looking through the lenses of politics and economics, it is also a serious mistake, for it prevents one from being able to see in three dimensions. To truly understand the significance of global events and trends, one must analyze them through a third lens as well: the lens of Scripture. Only then can the full picture become clearer."[168]

Ezekial 38 has a special place in Rosenberg's prophectic interpretations. The passage is a popular one for modern apocalyptic teachers. It speaks about the ruler of Gog and Magog (typically associated among prophecy teachers with Russia/ the former Soviet Union), threatening the restored nation of Israel. Through his "third lens" of analysis, Rosenberg sees this as a biblical prediction that the state of Russia, in alliance with Iran, will mount an offensive against the modern state of Israel. He associates nations (allied against Israel) mentioned in Ezekial 38, including Cush, Gomer and Put with the modern nations of Sudan, Ethiopia, Turkey, Germany, Libya and Algeria, among others.

---

[167] Joel C. Rosenberg. *Epicenter 2.0: Why the Current Rumblings in the Middle East Will Change Your Future* (Kindle), 79-82.
[168] Ibid, 738-740.

In light of his "third lens" view of current and future events, Rosenberg has created the Joshua Fund. The purpose of the "relief organization" is to support Israel's poor and victims of terrorism within the country and its occupied territories, based upon the special place of Israel in biblical prophecy. For evangelicals who have been persuaded by Rosenberg view of events and scripture, he presents the Joshua Fund as a means to fulfill the biblical mandate to "bless Israel" by, among other things:

- Praying for the peace of Jerusalem (Psalm 122:6)

- Praying knowledgeably and consistently for Israel and the Middle East

- Taking vision trips to-and attend conferences in-Israel and other Middle Eastern countries

- Publishing Christian books and music in Israel and the Middle East

- Investing in the rebuilding of Israel to welcome more Jewish people back to their ancient, God-given homeland

- Assisting the poor and needy in Israel

- Supporting the evangelical church in Israel and the Middle East as the only true hope for peace and reconciliation.[169]

Encompassed within Rosenberg's worldview, including the modern state of Israel and its Jewish population holding a special place in biblical prophecy, is the placement of the neighboring Muslim countries and their residents as the enemies of Israel. As such, Rosenberg suggests that they should be prayed for and loved, according to biblical mandate. Nonetheless, the Muslim peoples of the Middle East, as they are mentioned in *Epicenter,* are consistently

---

[169] Ibid, 2886-2893.

couched in the terms of "the enemy" of Israel and the Jews, and by prophetic extension, evangelical Christians.

A few years after Rosenberg published *Epicenter*, he completed his second major nonfiction work, *Inside the Revolution: How the Followers of Jihad, Jefferson & Jesus Are Battling to Dominate the Middle East and Transform the World*. This book offers evidence of a shift in Rosenberg's attitude toward Muslims in the Middle East.

In this book, Rosenberg places Muslims on the global stage into three categories: Radicals (including Al-Qaeda and Iranian Shiite activists), Reformers (Democracy-minded Muslims who oppose the Radicals), and the Revivalists (Muslims who accept Christ as Messiah and Son of God). Rosenberg's book is notable among evangelical literature on the topic because of its acknowledgment of the various streams of Islam, and the theological and historical background it provides for both Radical and Reformist Islamic movements. Much evangelical literature on the topic tends to treat modern Muslims as having a common agenda of global domination driven by a monolithic theology. In contrast, Rosenberg gives the reader clear snapshots of a variety of Islamic groups, along with the theological and historical underpinnings that are behind both militant and peaceful movements.

Rosenberg takes a novel approach when he discusses what he calls the Revivalists in the Muslims world. Those who fall under this term are former Muslims and nominal Christians who have become born-again believers. Rosenberg asserts that there is a burgeoning Christian movement in the Middle East, and Muslim leaders are worried that large numbers of Muslims are converting to Christianity. "There is now no question that so many people are becoming Christians in the region," wrote Rosenberg, "that Muslim leaders are becoming nervous and angry."[170] Rosenberg acknowledges that quantifying the actual depth of this revival is in the Middle East is very difficult.

---

[170] Joel C. Rosenberg, *Inside the Revolution* (Kindle), 6776-6777.

Like *Epicenter*, Rosenberg calls his Christian readers to action. However, the advice he gives for his evangelical audience seems to be the other side of the coin from his earlier work. That is, in *Epicenter*, his calls for action were Israel-focused, and gave a special place for Christian-Jewish relations. *Inside the Revolution* urges Christians to "show the love of Jesus Christ to their Muslim neighbors," in the following ways:

- Take Muslims new to your community a welcome gift

- Invite them to your home for dinner

- Be respectful of their customs, including taking off your shoes when you enter their home, refrain from alcohol, etc.

- Pray specifically for friends and family when eating with them, and don't be afraid to pray in the name of Jesus.

- Ask them about their culture and family

- Initiate activities that are fun and non–threatening to their faith before you consider asking them to a church service.

- When you make dinner for your family, consider making extra and taking it to your Muslim neighbor's house (no pork).

These and other suggestions reflect a broader outlook on Rosenberg's part toward Muslims. He sees embracing Muslims as both part of his call for evangelism as well as a fundamental directive of Christ's teachings:

"Today, there is no question that fear is preventing many followers of Jesus Christ from obeying His call to love the Muslim people. But others share Jonah's animosity toward the people of the epicenter," Rosenberg wrote. "We need to repent of such views. We need to ask God to change our hearts and give us His supernatural love. If we are ever going to join the Revolution—much less win it— the Church is going to need both courage and compassion." [171]

---

[171] Rosenberg,. *Inside the Revolution*, 8886-8889.

4
JESUS AND MAHDI: END TIMES FIGURES IN ISLAMIC HISTORY

Christian and Islamic eschatology contains a number of fascinating parallels with regard to the Second Coming of Jesus and the role of Antichrist. Their role in the historic development of these major religions has varied greatly over the ages. Yet, these beliefs continue to have an effect on how Muslims and Christians construct their responses to each other, and those responses help foster conflict or peaceful engagement.

In orthodox Christianity, Jesus contains two natures - both fully God and fully human. His divinity is described as being of the same substance as God the father, and being the "Word of God" that brought creation into being.[172] As the messiah, he is expected to return in the Last Days, defeat the Antichrist and set up an earthly kingdom that lasts for a thousand years.[173]

---

[172] John 1:1-4
[173] Revelation 20:4-6

Islam, however, vigorously disputes the idea that Jesus is God in the flesh. But there are some striking similarities between Islam and Christianity when it comes to the miraculous circumstances surrounding Jesus' birth as described in the Quran, the language that is used to describe him in Islamic literature, and the role he plays in Muslim eschatology. The development of Jesus as an end-time figure, along with other eschatological players can be traced from the Quran to Hadith, and on into Sufi, Shi'a and modern views.

Jesus in the Quran

Although the divinity of Jesus is rejected in Islam, there remain passages in the Quran that point to extraordinary circumstances surrounding his conception. A prime example is Surah 19:16-22:

> When [Mary] had withdrawn from her people to a chamber looking East, and had chosen seclusion from them. Then We sent unto her Our spirit and it assumed for her the likeness of a perfect man. She said: Lo! I seek refuge in the Beneficent One from thee, if thou art God fearing. He said: I am only a messenger of thy Lord, that I may bestow on thee a faultless son. She said: How can I have a son when no mortal hath touched me, neither have I been unchaste! He said: So (it will be). Thy Lord saith: It is easy for Me. And (it will be) that We may make of him a revelation for mankind and a mercy from Us, and it is a thing ordained. And she, conceived him...[174]

The following text presents Jesus as conceived, not through the participation of a human father, but through the breath of God: "And she who was chaste, therefore We breathed into her of Our spirit and made her and her son a token for all peoples." (21:90)

There are a number of passages in *Quran* that emphasize that God does not have "offspring." One such passage, perhaps designed to

---

[174] Marmaduke Pickthall, trans. *The Meaning of the Glorious Quran* (1930).

further separate the Jesus of Islam from the Jesus of Christianity, puts this statement in the mouth of Jesus himself:

"It befitteth not Allah to take unto himself a son. Glory be to Him! When He decreeth, He say unto it only: Be! And it is. And lo! Allah is my Lord and your Lord. So serve Him, that is the right path." (19:33-35)

The *Quran* also suggests that Jesus may have at one point overstepped his bounds in claims of divinity, and reemphasizes the Muslim belief in the one, wholly transcendent God. It also reveals a mistaken understanding of Mary and the Trinity:

> And when Allah saith: O Jesus, son of Mary! Didst thou say unto mankind: Take me and my mother for two gods beside Allah? he saith: Be Glorified! It was not mine to utter that which I had no right. If I used to say it, then Thou knewest it. Thou knowest what is in my mind, and I know not what is in Thy mind. Lo! Thou, only Thou art the Knower of Things Hidden. (5:116)

Other Quranic verses emphasize that Jesus (Isa) should be regarded by Muslims as no greater than other prophets that came before him, and does not have a divine nature (see: 4:157, 4:171, 5:74, 6:101, 19:90).

Jesus in Hadith and Other Writings

Outside the Quran, there is a body of *hadith* (sayings and deeds of Muhammad reported by his contemporaries) that deal with the character of Jesus and his role in history and the end times. One such *hadith* from Ahmad ibn Hanbal (with a similar account reported by Bukhari) tells of Muhammad's relationship with Jesus and his role in future events: "I am the closest of all the people to Jesus son of Mary, because there is no Prophet between him and myself. He will come again, and when you see him you will recognize him. He is of medium weight and his coloring is reddish white. He will be wearing two garments, and his hair will look wet. He will break the cross, kill the pigs, abolish the *jizya* (tax on non-Muslims) and call people to Islam. During this time, God will end every religion and sect other than Islam, and will destroy the Dajjal (Antichrist). Then peace and security will prevail on earth."[175] The passage tells of Jesus breaking the cross to emphasize that the crucifixion and resurrection of Christ as described in the Christian Gospels are not adhered to by the Muslim community.[176]

Other writings present textual parallels between stories told about Muhammad and those told of Jesus. Compare this eighth century passage from Abdallah ibn al-Mubarak with Surah 7:187:

> Mubarak: "Gabriel met Jesus and said to him, "Peace be upon you, Spirit of God." And upon you peace, Spirit of God," said Jesus. Then Jesus asked, "O Gabriel, when will the Hour come?" Gabriel's wings fluttered and he replied, "The questioned knows no more about this than the questioner. It has grown heavy in the heavens and the earth; it will only come upon you suddenly." Or else he said, "Only God will reveal it when it is time."[177]

> Quran: "They ask thee of the Hour, when will it come to port. Say: Knowledge thereof is with my Lord only. He alone will manifest it at its proper time. It is heavy in the heavens and the earth. It cometh not to you save unawares. They question thee as if thou couldst be well informed thereof. Say: Knowledge thereof is with Allah only, but most on mankind know not." (7:187)

Writing in the ninth century, Ahmad ibn Hanbal also tried to demonstrate the character of Jesus and his feeling about the final Day

---

[175] Muhammad 'Ata'ur-Rahim and Ahmad Thomson, *Jesus: Prophet of Islam*, 275.
[176] Ibid., 274.
[177] Tarif Khalidi, *The Muslim Jesus*, 54.

of Judgment: "Whenever the Hour was mentioned, Jesus used to cry out in anguish like a woman."[178]

The Role of Jesus in Future Events

Both Sunni and Shi'a Islam speak of the return of Jesus along with the coming "Mahdi," the restorer of religion and faith to the Islamic *ummah*. (The Mahdi is regarded as the Twelfth Imam in "twelver" Shi'ism). Among the points agreed upon by both main streams of Islam are that:

- The Mahdi will be a descendant of Muhammad through the line of Fatima,
- His coming will be accompanied by the appearance of the antichrist (Dajjal), and
- Arabs will take possession of their land from foreigners.[179]

In Shi'a Islam, the Twelfth Imam, Husayn, was both the political and spiritual head of the community. The end of his "occultation" as the Hidden Imam, bringing with him 72 former companions, will precede the return of Jesus.[180]

Among the *hadith* that describe Muhammad's interaction with Jesus during the night journey to Jerusalem are passages that describe Jesus defeating the Dajjal/Antichrist. As reported by Ahmad ibn Hanbal, Jesus said to Muhammad: "What my Lord told me is that the Dajjal will appear, and when he sees me he will begin to melt like lead. God will destroy him when he sees me. The Muslims will fight against the disbelievers, and the people will return to their own lands (Musnad, 1:375)."[181] Further writings tell of the period after the defeat of the

---

[178] Ibid., 74.
[179] Moojan Momen, *An Introduction to Shi'i Islam: The History and Doctrines of Twelver Shi'ism* (New Haven: Yale University Press, 1985) 168-169.
[180] Ibid., 170.
[181] Quoted in Rahim-Thomson, 271.

Dajjal that Jesus will marry and have children, and govern as a just ruler until his death.[182]

Sufis, Popular Religion and the Eschatology

The importance given to Jesus in Muslim eschatology closely resembles beliefs regarding the Mahdi. In the 14th century, the pioneering Muslim social historian Ibn Khaldun cast a critical eye toward end-times beliefs as he saw them develop. In the Muqaddimah, Ibn Khaldun writes: "It has been accepted by all Muslims in every epoch, that at the end of time a man from the family (of the Prophet) will without fail make his appearance ... Muslims will follow him, and he will gain domination over the Muslim realm ... After the Mahdi, Jesus will descend and kill the Antichrist."[183]

In his discussion of the return of Jesus and the Mahdi, Ibn Khaldun criticizes Sufis and popular religionists that advance the idea that the time of the Mahdi is near: "More recent Sufis have other theories concerning the Mahdi. The time, the man, and the place are clearly indicated in them. But the (predicted) time passes, and there is not the slightest trace (of the prediction coming true). Then some new suggestion is adopted." Also: "The common people, the stupid mass, who make claims with respect to the Mahdi ... assume that the Mahdi may appear in a variety of circumstances and places. They do not understand the real meaning of the matter."[184]

Some Muslim scholars find Shi'a or Sufi influence in messianic themes such as the Mahdi and the return of Jesus into Sunni Islam. Their criticism of the themes echoes Christian critics of dispensationalism. For example, modern scholar Fazlur Rahman wrote: "These doctrines, taken literally, are morally harmful is obvious; that they have actually caused incalculable harm to Muslim society is also a

---

[182] Ibid., 272.
[183] Ibn Khaldun, *The Muqaddimah*, 257-258.
[184] Ibid., 258-259.

CHRISTIANS AND MUSLIMS AT THE EPICENTER

glaring fact of history."[185] Rahman says that messianism of this sort "numbs the moral faculties and human initiative" and puts forth a pessimistic view of the world that things will only become worse as time goes on. He traces the adoption of these beliefs to eighth-century public preachers reaching out to the disillusioned and "morally starved masses."[186]

Mahdist Hopes in the Colonial Era

Popular movements regarding the Mahdi as a deliverer from the outside forces seem to resonate with people who are oppressed or fighting for liberation. Over the past 150 hundred years, some Muslim communities seeking to shed colonial domination have subscribed to the idea of a Mahdi-savior, and fight against the oppressors with the expectation that prosperity will follow. Like militant Muslim fundamentalists, Mahdism seeks to inaugurate a Golden Age of Islam.[187] Mahdist movements have been the driving force of for those fighting for liberation in places ranging from Algeria, to Sudan to Nigeria.[188] However, historians point out that as soon as the immediate crisis is over (i.e. Mahdist battles against the British in Sudan) the millennial reign of the Mahdi does not occur, and people usually return to a state of oppression or poverty.[189]

It is also noteworthy that Muslims fighting against Christian colonialists emphasize a Mahdi figure rather than Jesus as the one who conquers the antichrist. Perhaps the tendency was to not attach great importance to the central symbol of the of the colonialists' religion because it was more attractive to rally behind the exclusively Islamic concept of the Mahdi.

---

[185] Fazlur Rahman, *Islam,* 245.
[186] Ibid.
[187] Peter B. Clarke and Ian Linden, *Islam in Modern Nigeria*, 118.
[188] Ibid., 109.
[189] Ibid., 117.

Jesus and the Mahdi in Contemporary Thought

Today, there are both Christian and Muslim communities that closely follow world events and technological developments they feel support the hypothesis that the return of Jesus or the Mahdi will happen soon. The modern Shi'a scholar az-Zanjani says the advent of television fulfills the prophecy by the Sixth Imam that the Muslim brother in the east will be able to see his brother in the west.[190] Other Shi'a observers see the increasing political role of women and the encroachment of "permissible societies" into the Muslim world as further signs that the Hidden Imam will return soon.[191]

As some seek out signs of eschatological fulfillment, others are using figures such as Jesus and other prophets, including Muhammad, to help reform the Muslim view of how a society should be structured. Ali Abd al-Raziq, a jurist from Al-Azhar University, uses Jesus as a non-eschatological example for Muslims today. Al-Raziq argues that Islam does not demand a particular form of government, and that Muslims should seek to create democratic regimes. To support his argument, he points out that Jesus did not hold political leadership over his followers. Instead of a king, Jesus brought a message that could be enacted and carried out under a variety of political forms.[192]

The figure of Jesus as defined by Muslims since the time of Muhammad has variously been used to distinguish itself from Christianity and to bring hope to those looking for a deliverer. Writings from the Quran, the Hadith as well as Sufi and Shi'a literature demonstrate the importance of Jesus as a prophet of Islam. The Mahdi, also expected to appear shortly before of Jesus' return, has also become an important concept to both Sunni and Shi'a eschatological hopes.

---

[190] Momen, 166.
[191] Ibid., 167.
[192] 'Ali 'Abd al-Raziq, "Message Not Government, Religion Not State," 30.

5

LAND OF PROMISE OR DANGER ZONE: MUSLIMS IN THE U.S. BEFORE AND AFTER SEPTEMBER 11

The Muslim population is one of the fastest growing demographic groups in the United States. In addition to the challenges that all other burgeoning minorities face in finding a place in American society, Muslims have a religious and cultural history that has often been at odds with Western religious and cultural history. Many immigrant Muslims see America as a land of promise where economic opportunities abound. Americans often present the mix of cultures and religious groups existing in relative peace and stability as a model for nations around the world.

But there are also serious challenges that Muslim immigrants and their children in the U.S. must come to terms with as they establishing a presence here. Some of these issues are common to all groups of people that come to the United States; that is, assimilation vs. cultural preservation, overcoming stereotypes that often surround newcomers to the American scene, and developing a manner in which their concerns are heard in the political sphere.

Other issues that Muslims face surround the unique and, to many Muslim leaders, the all-encompassing role that religion plays in their life. They must also reconcile American foreign policy that may be seen, in the least, as antagonistic to some of their home countries, and at worst hostile to Islam itself.

There are several key issues that face Muslims in the United States: the preservation of Muslim identity in American culture, the challenge and nature of politics in a secular democracy, the role of Muslim women, and combating the effects of prejudice and discrimination.

On the one hand, America may become a land of promise where Muslims are free to prosper and practice their faith while participating fully in the American political and cultural milieu. On the other hand, the Muslim-American experience can be fraught with dangers such as prejudice, political marginalization, or a loss of moral cohesiveness. How well the American Muslim community, in particular those who are in the first few generations after immigration, succeeds in grasping that promise may depend greatly on how well these challenges are met.

Background

The history of Muslims in North America is often traced back to the moor Estevanico who traveled through the American southwest in the mid-16th century. The overlooked, but premier influx of a considerable number of Muslims into the United States came during the era of slavery. It is estimated that perhaps 10 percent of all the slaves brought to North America from North and West Africa were Muslim.[193] However, a lasting Muslim presence was not established through this population because slaves either adopted Christianity once

---

[193] Sulayman S. Nyang, "Christian-Muslim Dialogue in the United States," 330.

they reached North America, or their Muslim identity was otherwise lost in the succeeding generations.[194]

In the 20th century, Muslims have immigrated to the United States from all around the world, including Southeast Asia and Eastern Europe. Also worthy of note is the flow of Iranian migrants to the United States after the overthrow of the Shah in 1979.[195] The exact number of Muslims in the United States is a matter of debate, with estimates ranging from 1.3 million to more than seven million.[196]

Muslims often come to the U.S. seeking better educational opportunities, higher chances of economic prosperity, as well as religious and political freedoms that they do not find in their home country.[197] The major ethnic groups that make up America's immigrant Muslim population are Arabs, Indo-Pakistanis and Iranians. After immigrants, the next largest group is African-American Muslims, followed by the relatively small number of white converts.[198]

The first issue at hand is whether a Muslim can, according to Islamic law, be legally allowed to reside in a non-Muslim secular democracy such as the United States. Hardliners such as Sayyid Qutb said it is unthinkable to have a Muslim live outside a land without Islamic law and be subject to the laws of the unbelievers. "Any place where Islam is not dominant, becomes the home of hostility (dar-al-harb) for both the Muslims and the dhimmis [non-Muslims who agree to live in a Muslim state]. A Muslim must be prepared to fight against it, whether the country is his birthplace, a place where his relatives reside, or where his property or any other material interests are located."[199]

---

[194] Asma Gull Hasan, *American Muslims: The New Generation*, 17.
[195] Ibid., 47
[196] Kosmin, Barry A. and Ariela Keysar. *American Religious Identification Survey 2008*.
[197] Yvonne Yazbeck Haddad, "The Globalization of Islam, 606.
[198] Frederick Matthewson Denny, "The *Umma* in North America, 343.
[199] Sayyid Qutb, *Milestones*, 107-108.

However, the Egyptian jurist Rashid Rida asserts that there is nothing in Islam that prevents a Muslim from residing in a non-Muslim state providing that they are able to "manifest and practice their religion."[200] Rida argues that most countries that Muslims now live in do not qualify as the "Abode of Islam" (dar-al-Islam) in the classical sense, and therefore Islamic codes concerning civil and criminal law are not binding. He says that as a consequence, Muslims in these countries should pursue an empowering political and economic life.[201]

Cultural Preservation: The Mosque on Main Street

One of the fears that may haunt a Muslim immigrant is that the religious practices and cultural trappings they consider a part of their Muslim identity will gradually disappear as their children and grandchildren assimilate into American culture. In "The *Umma* in North America," Frederick Denny says that the fear of Muslims getting lost in the "melting pot" of America is an even greater fear than the challenges that arise from the many ethnic division that distinguish one American Muslim community from another.[202] He says that mosques often serve as common places of worship for Muslims of different ethnicities, but these groups often go their separate ways when the worship service is over.[203]

The number of mosques in the United States has risen greatly as the Muslim population has increased over the past few decades. The mosque functions as the Islamic community's social hub, a center for Islamic education and a kind of safe haven from the pressures of non-Muslim America.[204]

Muslim jurists and other thinkers have debated about the degree to which the Muslim community should be isolated from American

---

[200] Khaled Abou El Fadl, "Striking a Balance, 49.
[201] Ibid., 55.
[202] Denny, 349.
[203] Ibid., 345
[204] Yvonne Yazbeck Haddad, "The Globalization of Islam, 619.

society in order to retain its Muslim character. One Moroccan Islamist, Ali Kettani, suggests that in order to create a truly Islamic community in North America, Muslims should organize themselves into "enclaves," where aspects of life such as education, finance, Islamic practice and language, etc. could be preserved.[205] The founder of Pakistan's leading Islamist political and religious party (Jama'at-i-Islami) Abdul Ala Mawdudi encouraged Muslims to avoid integration with Western society "lest they lose their souls in the West's wayward ways."[206]

However, some oppose the idea of cutting the American Muslim community off from their non-Muslim neighbors. Muhammad Abdul Rauf of the Islamic Center of Washington insists that America, while dominated by the Judeo-Christian traditions, is a staunch guardian of an individual's right to pursue their faith as they choose.[207]

Discrimination - The Muslim Next Door

One of the pressures Muslims face in the United States is prejudice and misunderstanding from their non-Muslim neighbors. In *American Muslims: A New Generation*, Asma Gull Hasan says the greatest challenge for Muslims is to overcome their public image as terrorists.[208] Hasan says that one reason people in the United States quickly adopt anti-Muslim or anti-Arab stereotypes is because Islam and what Muslims are all about is very much a mystery to the general public.[209] A fountain of misunderstanding about Islam is also found between America's two main religious groups, Christians and Jews. Jewish Americans often have political and familial interest in the state of Israel, which puts them at odds with many Arabs who have political, familial and ideological ties with Palestinians. As mentioned earlier,

[205] Yvonne Yazbeck Haddad, "The Dynamics of Islamic Identity," 28.
[206] Yvonne Yazbeck Haddad, "The Globalization of Islam, 612.
[207] Ibid.
[208] Hasan, 28.
[209] Ibid., 86.

some conservative Christian groups potentially see Muslims as agents of the Antichrist.[210]

American Muslim organizations such as the Council on American-Islamic Relations (CAIR) are engaged documenting accounts of violence and discrimination. Many Muslims remember the harassment that followed the Oklahoma City bombing until it was determined that it was an act of a domestic, non-Muslim terrorist.[211] Others say slanted news reports and coverage concentrating on militant fundamentalists creates a false impression about what most Muslims are about.[212]

Some see better-qualified journalists as being an important part of raising the quality of how of Muslims are portrayed in the news media. Others envision the greater integration of Muslims into the American educational apparatus as a key component of creating a better understanding of Muslims in the United States. Shahid Athar says the "teaching of Islam in universities and colleges should be done more seriously and not superficially ... At a freshmen or a junior level, one hardly gets exposure to the religion of Islam and his or her knowledge of the religion is usually derived from the way it is projected in the media."[213]

The Debate Among Muslim Women

Perhaps the most visible representative of the Muslim community in America is the observant Muslim woman who covers her head with a *hijab*. Western assumptions about women in Islam often portray them as oppressed and subjugated in a male-dominated religion and culture. Among non-Muslim westerners, the *hijab* is sometimes seen as a symbol of all that is wrong with the status afforded to women under

[210] Yvonne Yazbeck Haddad, "The Globalization of Islam, 626.
[211] Jane I. Smith, *Islam in America,* 175.
[212] Greg Noakes, "Striking a Balance," 287.
[213] Shahid Athar, *Reflections of an American Muslim,* (Chicago: Kazi Publications, 1994), 69.

Islam, and a visible reminder that someone different and foreign is in their midst. However, many Muslim women consider the *hijab* an integral part of their faith, and a means of maintaining their dignity as a person by not appearing as a sex object to men.[214] It must be noted that not all Muslim women choose to wear a head covering, and some see it as an extra-religious cultural trait that is their choice whether or not to carry over into American public life.[215]

In "The Hijab and Religious Liberty," Kathleen Moore cites several lawsuits between women who chose to wear the head covering and their employers who forbade it. In one case, a retirement home operated by a Presbyterian ministry did not allow a receptionist to cover because it represented non-Christian belief at a Christian organization. In another case, a Philadelphia public school district would not hire a Muslim woman because she would not agree to remove her headscarf during work hours.[216]

Sharifa Alkhateeb of the North American Women's Council says that Muslim women often feel like easy targets because they are identified quickly as being a member of a minority group misunderstood by the American public. She says, "Sometimes people will tell [Muslim women wearing a scarf] 'go back where you came from.' For myself, I'll say I was born here, you know I'm not going anywhere. This is my country too."[217]

Alkhateeb says that shortly after the September 11th terrorist attacks, she considered taking off her *hijab* to avoid standing out so clearly as a Muslim. "September 12 I took off my scarf and put on a cap that covered all my hair, and my neck was open, and I put on a high collar. But I felt very uncomfortable because it wasn't me. And I decided on the second day that it is not worth doing. Why should I

---

[214] Hasan, 128.
[215] Maha Alkhateeb, interview with the author, February 2002.
[216] Kathleen Moore, "The Hijab and Religious Liberty," 107.
[217] Sharifa Alkhateeb, interview with the author, February 2002.

turn myself inside out like that just to make myself acceptable to someone who wants to hate me?"[218]

She also recognizes that, while there are those in the United States who want to persecute people they do not understand, there is also growing interest in the among many Americans to learn more about Islam and Muslim society. She says, "We know the books in Muslim bookstores are flying off the shelves. We know that people are trying hard to understand more about Muslims, whether because they hate Muslims or they just want to know and understand more and don't have a clue."[219]

However her daughter, Maha Alkhateeb, chooses not wear the *hijab,* and considers herself a devout Muslim woman. She also says, especially since the September 11th attacks, pressures on women like her reach beyond the issue of traditional clothing. Maha says that as both Muslim women and men move through non-Muslim American society, they often feel conspicuous, "You look different. Your name is funny, you come from a funny religion, you are not one of us. So something I found ironic after September 11 is that people are like 'grab your flag, jump on the bandwagon, you can be American now, it's okay.' You have to show your patriotism."[220]

Maha says that despite the pressures that come with being Arab and Muslim in America, she values the diverse cultural experience that her son is experiencing. "I like the fact that my child has Muslim friends and Christian friends, and Arab friends and Asian friends, and white American and African American [friends]." She also says that it is often easier to be a good Muslim as a woman in the United States because she can practice her religion without what she regards as the patriarchal baggage that is part of some Muslim countries, including her former home of Saudi Arabia.[221]

---

[218] Ibid.
[219] Ibid.
[220] Maha Alkhateeb interview.
[221] Ibid.

Unity in the Midst of Diversity

Perhaps one of the greatest challenges before the American Muslim community is the need to have a voice in the American political process. It must be understood that Muslims in the United States come from a wide variety of national, economic and cultural backgrounds. Arab Muslims from countries such as Saudi Arabia, Kuwait and Iraq may find some commonality when establishing themselves in America, but it might take an extra amount of effort to form similar bonds with Pakistanis, Indonesians or sub-Saharan African Muslims.

In his study of the Muslim population of Indianapolis, Steve Johnson observed that the major divisions among Muslims in that city fall along lines of conservative vs. liberal, socioeconomic status and immigrant vs. indigenous adherents. He also notes that among indigenous, African-American Muslims, there is an additional split between those who follow Warith Deen Muhammad and those who follow Louis Farrakhan.[222]

Certainly the struggle between Israelis and Palestinians is a uniting force for Muslims around the world, including the United States. Many American Muslims would like their voices heard as U.S. foreign policy is formed on this issue. But participation in the American democratic process also entails the ability of Muslims to influence local issues such as zoning rights for mosques, the establishment of Muslim schools and legal protections to stave off discrimination.

On the national level, a unified political voice may lend more credibility to American Muslims when it comes to foreign policy decisions about (and often against) Muslim countries. It is a common criticism that the average non-Muslim in America is not fully aware of the actions of its own government in places such as Israel/the

---

[222] Steve A. Johnson, "The Muslims of Indianapolis," 274.

Palestinian territory, Afghanistan and the Persian Gulf, and how it has an often profound effect on the people who live there. Shahid Athar says that American Muslims hold a special role in informing the American public about U.S. foreign policy as it relates to the Muslim world. Athar writes: "We should be able to educate fellow Americans about the sufferings of Muslims in Muslim countries and be able to explain why they are being oppressed. We also need to express our solidarity with Muslims in Muslim countries in a justifiable cause ... We should coordinate our efforts to have a better impact rather than a hundred different organizations doing the same thing."[223]

Mohammed Muqtedar Khan points to the American Muslim Council (AMC) as one group that is "trying to draw inclusive circles to generate power based on numbers by creating the identity of American Muslims."[224]

In *Islam in America*, Jane Smith says different immigrant groups have squabbled among themselves. "Some newly arrived Pakistanis, for example, may think second- and third- generation Arab Muslims are too liberal, and the Arabs in response may resent the 'bossy' way in which the Pakistanis tell them how to be Muslim."[225] Smith and others also point out that the rift between Shi'a and Sunni Muslims often translates into a dividing factor when it comes to organizing the diverse American Muslim community into a unified voice in the public square.[226]

The difficulties faced by American Muslims on the political scene is exacerbated by the fact that they do not have much in the way powerful allies as some other minority groups have in the United States (i.e. the Christian Right's relationship with the Jewish lobby on the issue of Israel).

---

[223] Athar, 90-91.
[224] Mohammed A. Muqtedar Khan, "Muslims and Identity Politics in America," 90.
[225] Jane I. Smith, *Islam in America*, 181.
[226] Ibid.

The American Muslim Community after September 11th

The American cultural landscape became more treacherous for the American Muslim after the September 11th terrorist attacks. The challenges before the attacks have not gone away, and in some instances are now placed in high relief. Also, the effort to root out terrorist cells and collaborators within the United States by the American government has left many Muslims afraid of unjust imprisonment or harassment.[227]

On March 20, 2002, federal agents raided the homes and offices of Muslims living in Virginia and Georgia. The raids were part of the Treasury Department's effort to cut off funding from the United States for terrorists associated with Osama bin Laden. Those who were caught in the raids said agents with guns invaded their homes, handcuffed them and rifled through personal belongings looking for evidence.[228]

Also, instances ranging from harassment to outright attack also heighten fears in the American Muslim community. One such attack occurred on March 25, 2002 when a man drove his pick-up truck into a Tallahassee, Florida mosque. Police say the perpetrator, Charles D. Franklin, was motivated by hatred of Muslims and had previously tried to join the military in order to "kill Muslims."[229]

Organizations such as the Council on American-Islamic Relations (CAIR) document incidents of discrimination and violence against the American Muslim community. They also are active in advocating Muslim issues and informing the media, Congress and other organizations about how Muslims are perceived and treated in the United States. On April 30, 2002 CAIR released a report on the status

---

[227] Judith Miller, "U.S. Raids Continue, Prompting Protests," *The New York Times* 21 March 2002.

[228] Jennifer Hoyt, "Muslim Groups Criticize US Raids," Associated Press, 21 March 2002.

[229] Council on America-Islamic Relations, "Florida Mosque Attack Result of Anti-Muslim Rhetoric," 26 March 2002.

of Muslim civil rights in the United States. The report concluded that government actions such as the raids described above have created an atmosphere among American Muslims where they are "are more apprehensive than ever about discrimination and intolerance."[230]

In addition to a long list of incidents that may constitute harassment or discrimination by individuals and businesses, the CAIR report also criticizes the U.S. government the use of secret evidence to detain Muslims and to justify sanctions against Muslim organizations suspected of terrorist links.[231] The organization also says that a number of Muslims who were interrogated by the FBI subsequently lost their jobs because of what they call the "targeting" of Arabs and Muslims.[232]

Further criticism of the American government comes in response to the USA Patriot Act of 2001. CAIR characterizes the act as giving "the executive branch the power to detain immigrant suspects for lengthy periods of time, sometimes indefinitely," and allowing "the executive branch to circumvent the Fourth Amendment's requirement of probable cause when conducting wiretaps and searches."[233]

But as some see the pendulum swinging toward jeopardized Muslim civil rights, there are mechanisms within the American judicial framework that may serve to prevent these civil rights from evaporating.. One of the actions that the Muslim community finds most disturbing after the September 11th attacks is the imprisoning of Muslims and Arabs without filing formal charges. In the Justice Department's pursuit of Osama bin Laden's links in the U.S., hundreds were detained on immigration charges unrelated to the government's terrorism investigation, as well as a number not charged with a crime but still held in high security prisons as material witnesses.[234] The

---

[230] Council on American-Islamic Relations, *The Status of Muslim Civil Rights in the United States*, 3.
[231] Ibid., 1.
[232] Ibid., 8.
[233] Ibid., 4.
[234] Steve Fainaru and Amy Goldstein, "Judge Rejects Jailing of Material Witnesses," *The Washington Post*, 30 April 2002, A01.

Justice Department argues that those detained, but not charged, are being correctly held under the rarely invoked material witness statute last updated by Congress in 1984.[235]

During the first week of May 2002, a federal judge ruled that the jailing of material witnesses overreaches the Justice Department's authority, and also dismissed charges against a Jordanian student accused of perjury.[236] Judge Shira A. Scheindlin wrote, "If the government has probable cause to believe a person has committed a crime, it may arrest that person…But since 1789, no Congress has granted the government the authority to imprison an innocent person in order to guarantee that he will testify before a grand jury conducting a criminal investigation."[237]

Before the September 11th attacks, the Muslim community in the United States faced a series of daunting challenges in the quest to the find stability, prosperity and the kind of participation in public life that other minorities enjoy. The place of Muslim law in secular society, the preservation of the Muslim community, how to look after the interests of the worldwide Muslim community in a country such as the U.S., as well as the struggle against misunderstanding and prejudice are critical themes in the life of American Muslims.

Following the September 11th attacks, many Muslim claim they are unduly targeted, not only by their neighbors who may not understand them well, but also by a government that is reacting unjustly in the name of a war against terrorism.[238]

Anticipating a backlash, President Bush called on Americans shortly after September 11th to not confuse the religion of Islam with the actions of the terrorists. Bush also appeared with Muslim religious and political leaders from time to time since then. President Barack Obama has made a series of significant overtures to Muslims around

---

[235] Ibid.
[236] Ibid.
[237] Ibid.
[238] CAIR 2002, 16.

the world as well as in the United States. However, the danger and alienation that Muslim immigrants are experiencing as the U.S. responds to September 11th may tend to make the promises that America holds for them look somewhat more elusive than they once appeared.

6

MUSLIM ENCOUNTERS IN THE EVANGELICAL PRESS: 1996 TO 2001

Introduction

The core of this report is how the September 11th attacks have changed how evangelicals view and discuss the issue of Islam and encounters with Muslims. Tracking the changes in overall evangelical discourse toward Muslims can be somewhat difficult given the diversity of members in the evangelical family.[239] However, a key feature of American evangelicalism, its multi-million dollar publishing industry, offers a window into how the various members on the evangelical "family farm" are nourishing their ideologies and reactions to the changing environment. This chapter will examine news coverage prior to 2001 in evangelical magazines, tracking how the movement is adapting, and the what kind of fruit certain attitudes and behavior may bear with respect to Muslim-Christian encounters.

---

[239] Robert D. Woodberry and Christian S. Smith, "Fundamentalism Et Al: Conservative Protestants in America," 25-56.

Borrowing from the field of sociaology, the approach of "framing processes" and calls to action in social movement organizations (SMO's) provides a valuable tool in analyzing the emergence of Islam and Muslims in the scope of the evangelical discourse. Sociologists Robert Benford and David Snow devised a theory of how certain framing processes are used by SMO's to draw adherents, encourage beliefs and elicit action.[240]

Evangelicalism does not fit the full definition of an SMO because it is not a clearly defined organization with a set agenda, nor do its members always agree on social and ecclesiastical goals of the movement. Therefore, within the realm of frame analysis, evangelicalism may fit the category of an "unmobilized sentiment pool" or "public opinion preference cluster," from which various theologically-conservative SMO's may seek to draw participants.[241]

However, certain frame alignment processes are at work within evangelicalism, and that they can be identified through examining press reports produced by the evangelical community. Those processes include "frame bridging," by the use of mass media to introduce a new idea or message within the framework of evangelical ideology, "frame amplification" of certain values that those in editorial or activist leadership roles desire to infuse into the sentiment pool, and "frame extension" of situations and concerns that at first glance may have little direct bearing on the daily lives of those within American evangelicalism.[242]

The most significant framing trends presented in this chapter are in the categories of conflict and dialogue. In the case of conflict, the articles appearing in Christian publications between 1996 and 1998 point to the following themes:

---

[240] David A. Snow, E. Burke Rochford, et al., "Frame Alignment Processes, Micromobilization, and Movement Participation," 464-481.

[241] Ibid., 467.

[242] Ibid., 467-472.

a) Evangelicals are spiritually connected to Christians of all types living in the developing world,

b) Christians in these countries are often persecuted and experience constraints on religious freedom, and

c) Outside China, the most widespread group persecuting Christians are Muslims and Muslim-dominated governments.

The following look at evangelical press coverage will include an examination of articles that collectively present an "injustice frame" about religious conflicts around the world.[243] In terms of social action, the conflict articles build the ideological underpinnings that evangelical activists may use to elicit support for certain causes (i.e. legislation making religious freedom advocacy a part of U.S. foreign policy). However, the press coverage in this time period remains within the purview of forming ideas within a "sentiment pool," while on occasion seeking to mobilize readers into action. (This changes somewhat in the press coverage following the Sept. 11 attacks.)

In the case of dialogue, the data that follows reflects a much different stream of thought toward interfaith encounters. Articles in the years preceding 2001 show a few evangelicals promoting the idea of friendly and cooperative relationships with Muslims, as well as their desire to increase theological and cultural understanding. In this case, the framing of Christian-Muslim interaction does not necessarily betray a desire for a specific political goal. Rather, social and spiritual goals are cited, including more opportunities proselytize and the ability to maintain a presence in communities where Christians feel the threat of marginalization. In the category of "dialogue," the following survey of evangelical press coverage will show that advocates of friendly and

---

[243] Robert D. Benford, David A. Snow, "Framing Processes and Social Movements," 615.

inquisitive encounters between Muslims and Christians also create a "collective action frame," but outside the realm of an "injustice frame" as described by Benford and Snow.[244]

Christianity Today Magazine

The primary focus will be on evangelicalism's paper of record, *Christianity Today*. The magazine is the flagship publication of Christianity Today International, which publishes ten other magazines with titles ranging from *Books & Culture* to *Christian History & Biography*. The company also produces an extensive website, linking the various publications under a single web presence and posting a large number of stories and discussion forums independent of its print products. As for *Christianity Today* (CT), the magazine claims a readership of more than 340,000, with a paid circulation of 155,000.[245] The magazine says the median age of its readers is about 53 years old, more than two thirds of which are men. Also, more than a quarter of the readers are said to be clergy members. Readers of CT appear to be very well educated: more than 80 percent are college graduates, and more than half have graduate degrees.[246]

Like many institutions within the evangelical establishment, *Christianity Today* traces its heritage to evangelist Billy Graham. In the mid-1950's Graham and others, including Carl F.H. Henry, L. Nelson Bell, Harold Ockenga and philanthropist J. Howard Pew, set out to create a magazine that would advance a decidedly evangelical worldview, using the mainline journal *Christian Century* as the model.[247] Graham reportedly envisioned the magazine as planting "the evangelical flag in the middle of the road, taking a conservative theological position but a classic liberal approach to social problems. It

[244] Ibid.
[245] Advertising Rates and Data, *Christianity Today Magazine*.
[246] Ibid.
[247] Marsden, 158.

would combine the best in liberalism and the best in fundamentalism without compromising theologically."[248] The launch of *Christianity Today* in 1956, with Carl Henry at the helm as editor, has been credited as adding a "measure of cohesiveness" to the evangelical movement while it was still in its infancy.[249]

Sojourners Magazine

While *Christianity Today* will be examined as the centerpiece publication, this chapter will also review other evangelical periodicals where the content falls either to the left or right on the political spectrum, even though they hold similar theological positions. *Sojourners Magazine*, a publication out of Washington, DC has been selected as a long-established publication that describes itself as "a Christian ministry whose mission is to proclaim and practice the biblical call to integrate spiritual renewal and social justice."[250] *Sojourners* is the successor to a magazine called *The Post-American* produced in the early 1970's by a group of Trinity Evangelical Divinity School students opposed to the Vietnam War. These students later moved to Washington, DC to live and work in the low-income area of Columbia Heights in the nation's capital. The young evangelicals involved in the group lived communally; drawing from a common budget and living in mutually shared housing.[251] Another example of this type of Christian community springing from the Jesus Movement of the early 1970's is Jesus People USA in Chicago. JPUSA remains an active community, providing similar social services as the *Sojourners* community. It also produced a publication called *Cornerstone*. However, *Cornerstone Magazine* had a much less political focus than *Sojourners*, and ceased publication in 2003.

---

[248] Ibid.
[249] Ahlstrom, 958.
[250] Mission Statement, *Sojourners Magazine*.
[251] History, *Sojourners: Faith Politics and Culture*.

In contrast, by 2003 the Sojourners community had grown beyond its roots in communal Christian living and formed an "intentional community" with a "common rule of life." The neighborhood center that was begun in the mid-1970's was reorganized into a more traditional not-for-profit organization, and many of the current staff have not participated in the communal aspects of the group.[252] However, the Sojourners ministry has cultivated a distinct political and social dimension to its theologically-conservative outlook. A key example of *Sojourners'* political and theological orientation is found in the June 2004 cover story "No Place to Stand," which discusses the dilemma of theologically-conservative Christians who are opposed to abortion rights, but otherwise hold a "progressive" political outlook.[253]

World Magazine

World Magazine began its run in 1986 as a successor to the *Southern Presbyterian Journal,* which was started in the 1940's as a voice of conservatism within the Presbyterian Church-United States denomination.[254] The founder of the *Journal* was L. Nelson Bell, who also worked with his son-in-law, evangelist Billy Graham, in the founding of *Christianity Today.*[255] *World* is published by God's World Publishing in Asheville, North Carolina, and is cited as having a paid subscriber base of more than 124,000.[256] As shown in the following survey of coverage, *World* retains a staunchly conservative theological and political outlook.

---

[252] Ibid.

[253] Heidi Schlumpf, "No Place to Stand," 12-16.

[254] A brief History of the World Journalism Institute.
http://www.worldji.com/history.asp

[255] "Papers of Lemuel Nelson Bell - Collection 318," Billy Graham Center Archives, Wheaton College.

[256] Audit Bureau of Circulations, 31 December 2003.

The analysis of Christianity Today's articles that fall under the category of Christian-Muslim interaction covers the years 1996 through 2003. In all, 202 articles gleaned from the CT archives fit the criteria that they were printed in the magazine (as opposed to online-only pieces), and dealt with Muslims or the religion of Islam. In compiling and categorizing these articles, it became apparent that the nature of the CT articles fell into one of four categories:

(a) Muslim-Christian Conflict

This category contains news stories or commentary that deals with physical, legal or theological clashes between Muslims and Christians. The most common form of "conflict" article is that of religious violence between Muslims and Christians in various hot spots around the world. It should be noted that this category does not indicate the promotion of conflict by the CT editors, or necessarily report instances out of proportion to actual events. Rather, the conflict category is used to distinguish how much the topic enters evangelical discourse in the magazine.

(b) Context and Understanding

This category encompasses articles that help the Christian reader get a clearer sense of what defines Islam, Muslim life in the United States and abroad, or the context of a region where Muslims and Christians are living together under duress (i.e. the Middle East).

(c) Mission and Evangelism

This category covers articles about efforts to convert Muslims to Christianity, as well as relief efforts by evangelical agencies.

(d) Dialogue

This category involves those articles that advocate, or report on, non-conversion oriented cooperation between Muslims and Christians.

Due to each magazine's respective editorial approaches, the articles from the *Sojourners* and *World* do not fit into these same categories. Also, the amount of reporting and commentary on Islam and Muslim-Christian encounters done in these two publications is much less than in CT. Therefore a direct comparison between the three magazines might not be useful using the categories described above. However, after an in-depth look into CT's reporting, a summary of articles on the subject from the other two magazines will provide a wider understanding of the currents within evangelicalism as they relate to Islam and Muslims.

Muslim-Christian Encounters in *Christianity Today*:

The following charts below illustrate *Christianity Today* coverage pertaining to Islam and/or Muslims from 1996 through 2003:

Article Category Frequency by Year

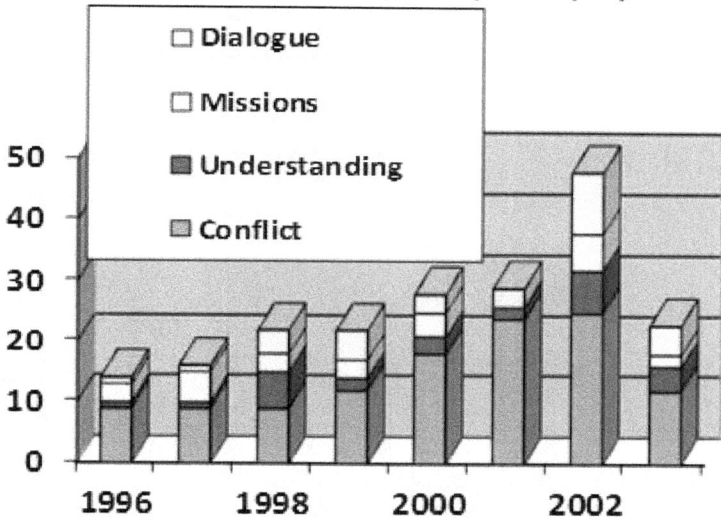

Legend:
- □ Dialogue
- □ Missions
- ■ Understanding
- ▨ Conflict

Number of Words by Year

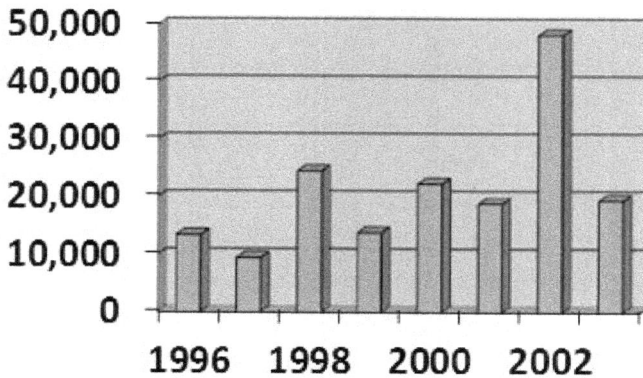

Total Articles by Category 1996-2003:

Conflict = 118 Dialogue = 32

Understanding = 27 Missions/Evangelism = 25

1996: Rumblings of Persecution

Total Articles: 14

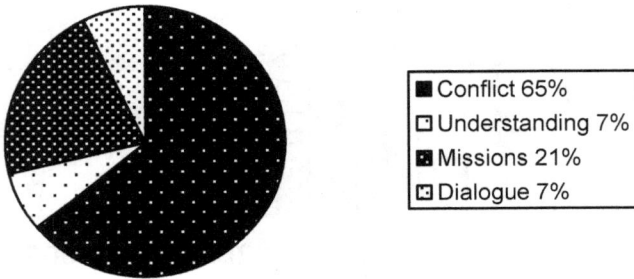

Legend:
- Conflict 65%
- Understanding 7%
- Missions 21%
- Dialogue 7%

Conflict: 9   Understanding: 1   Missions: 3   Dialogue: 1

Conflict

The number of articles published in 1996 on Muslim-Christian encounters is relatively few compared to coverage just a few years later. However, the trend of conflict outnumbering all other categories is established from this year onward. One of the most significant items in this category is a 3,920-word article by Kim A. Lawton on the persecution of Christians around the world. The article was prompted by a "Statement of Conscience" by the National Association of Evangelicals, which according to the editors of CT, "came at a time of little concern for religious persecution."[257] It touches on non-Muslim areas such as China, Vietnam and Latin America. However, the main

---

[257] Kim A. Lawton, "The Suffering Church," *Christianity Today*, 15 July 1996.

focus is on the problems evangelicals and other Christians face in the Muslim world.

The piece begins with the story of "Robert" Hussein Qambar Ali, a Kuwaiti citizen to whom an Islamic court recommended the death penalty for his conversion to Christianity. It also focuses on a Dutch missionary called Brother Andrew, famous for once smuggling Bibles behind the Iron Curtain. Brother Andrew is noted in the article for shifting the focus of his work toward Muslim countries after the fall of the Soviet Union.

The article quotes an unnamed Arab Christian leader as saying "Muslim extremists vary their attacks, sometimes seeing their main enemy as Israel, sometimes secularism and materialism of the West, sometimes the Crusades, and sometimes proselytism and missionary efforts." "Evangelicals have been particular targets," he adds, because they are seen as being tied to 'all of the above.'"[258] The article also cites a scholar at a conservative think tank, the Hudson Institute, as drawing parallels between the scapegoating of Jews in 19th century Europe and the blame heaped upon Christians in the non-Western world at the end of the 20th century.

The article's language also sets the stage for the evangelical response to Muslims by highlighting the issue of Christian persecution. The article points to a new effort by the NAE to push for U.S. legislation that promotes religious liberty around the world, improves the State Department's documentation of religious persecution, and imposes sanctions against countries that oppress religious minorities.

The article also points to "strategies apart from politics," including the call for more evangelicals to get involved in the promotion of human rights. The article ends on a quote from Brother Andrew, calling for "friendship evangelism" by Christians among Muslims. "We must forever set aside the idea that they are our enemies ... We did this for decades with the Russians – they were terrible, evil communists

---

[258] Ibid.

who were going to conquer the world. That very attitude on our part is why it took so long for their system to crumble. In our fear we did not go to them with the love of God."[259]

In an Easter column, Chuck Colson mirrored some of the same concerns about persecution of Christians around the world as Lawton's expose, with an emphasis on countries such as Sudan, Pakistan, Saudi Arabia and Egypt. Examples of persecution range from forced conversion by Sudanese troops on behalf of the Muslim government to the abduction and assassination of three evangelical pastors in Iran. At the end of the article, Colson issues a call to political action: "It is time for us to use our pulpits and publications to cry out in defense of fellow believers. Each of us can write our political leaders demanding that they reform INS policy and make persecution of Christians a priority when negotiating with other countries."[260]

In late April, an editorial by CT Editor David Neff called for the evangelical community to pray for those Christians persecuted in primarily Muslim countries. Neff also mentioned the effort by the National Association of Evangelicals to influence State Department and Immigration and Naturalization Service policy toward those seeking asylum in the United States based on religious persecution. Neff maintained that diplomats negotiating in countries where persecution exists are frequently not fully briefed on the problem, and that "too often economic considerations are allowed to trump religious liberty as American corporations press for free trade with oppressive countries."[261] Neff framed the common Christian experience as being that of persecution, with the religious freedom and political clout experienced in the United States as a "parenthesis of toleration" in a world where fellow believers are suffering.[262]

---

[259] Ibid.

[260] Charles Colson, "Tortured for Christ," *Christianity Today*, March 1996.

[261] David Neff, " Our Extended, Persecuted Family," *Christianity Today*, 29 April, 1996, 14.

[262] Ibid.

In subsequent months, conflict articles included news briefs on church burnings in Indonesia.[263] Another short news item (running 70 words) appeared on the acquittal of three Muslims, including at least one cleric, in the 1994 murder of a Pakistani Christian outside a courthouse in Lahore. The 20-year-old victim, who died of a head wound, was reported as being a defendant in a case where he was accused of blaspheming the prophet Muhammad (the cleric acquitted of his murder was the plaintiff in the blasphemy case).[264]

Conflict articles also included a report on the efforts to sign a peace accord with Muslim separatist groups in the Philippines and an editorial by a Croatian evangelical leader on ethno-religious violence in Bosnia.[265]

Among the conflict articles in 1996, one seemed critical of an evangelical group called Christian Peacemaker Teams (CPT). The group consists of mostly Mennonite, Brethren and Quaker members, and was started by Ron Sider, the founder of Evangelicals for Social Action.[266] The article says CPT's mission is nonviolent intervention in international conflicts, in this case the troubled West Bank town of Hebron.

The article reported all the members of CPT in Hebron were arrested by Israeli authorities when they attempted to uproot olive tree seedlings recently planted by Jewish settlers near Hebron. The article also says CPT members claimed they were assaulted by Jewish settlers as they tried to establish homes in the Palestinian territory. Though CPT claims neutrality, Jewish leaders criticized the group for siding

---

[263] "Muslim Mobs Destroy Churches," *Christianity Today*, 16 September 1996, 112. "Church Burnings: Muslim Mobs Kill Five in Indonesia," *Christianity Today*, 11 November 1996, 96.

[264] "News Briefs," *Christianity Today*, 15 July 1996, 65.

[265] David Reid Miller, "Philippines: Muslim Separatists Sign Peace Accord," *Christianity Today*, 28 October 1996, 81. Peter Kuzmic, "Editorial: Bosnia's Bitter Truths."

[266] Timothy C. Morgan, "Hebron's Peacemakers Find No Shalom in Olive Branches," *Christianity Today*, 16 September 1996, 92.

with Palestinians and not taking an even-handed approach in dealing with Arab-Jewish conflict in the region. One settler is said, "This group, instead of making shalom between Arabs and Jews, is making war between us - and this is a great pity."[267]

Understanding

The single article in the category of Understanding also deals with the encounters between Muslims and Christians in the Palestinian Territories and Israel. In an article called "Jerusalem's Living Stones," Timothy Morgan outlined some of the various Christian groups that live in Jerusalem, from Arab Christians to Messianic Jews, and some of the tensions they face in the Israeli-Palestinian conflict. In particular, he cited numerous examples of Western Christians subscribing to popular notions about the role of Israel in the end times, and the rift those notions create between Arab Christians and evangelicals. Also, he noted efforts by some evangelical organizations to point toward the threat of Muslim extremism as the chief threat against the historic church in Jerusalem, rather than the rise in both the Jewish and Muslim populations in the city, and the precipitous drop in the Christian population due to a number of other circumstances.[268]

Missions/Evangelism

Three articles fit the category of missions and evangelism during 1996. The first profiled a Greek Cypriot missionary named Spiros Zodhiates, who is noted for his founding of the American Mission to Greeks, as well as his large church planting efforts in predominantly

---

[267] Ibid.
[268] Timothy C. Morgan, "Jerusalem's Living Stones," *Christianity Today*, 20 May 1996, 58.

Muslim countries such as Indonesia.[269] The second was a news update on Hussein Qambar Ali, who at the time was flown out of Kuwait through the help of Christian Solidarity International (CSI), described as a interdenominational human-rights group helping persecuted Christians. The third article was penned by author Steve Rabey, who wrote abut a gathering of church and parachurch leaders who met in Colorado Springs to discuss evangelization strategies for the Muslim world. Rabey's article says there was much disagreement about effective forms of missions, with dividing lines between, for example, the use of conversion-oriented satellite broadcasts and the participation of U.S. government pressure to protect indigenous Christians.[270]

Dialogue

The single article in 1996 that falls into the category of dialogue deals with a group of evangelical Christians who retraced the steps of the Crusaders in a "Reconciliation Walk." The point of the walk was to "build bridges of understanding and to reverse a legacy of animosity" between Christians and Muslims. The participants in the walk were offering apologies to Muslims for the behavior of Christians in the Middle Ages, saying Crusaders "betrayed the name of Christ by conducting themselves in a manner contrary to his wishes and character." The effort was praised by George Washington University professor Seyyed Hossein Nasr: "Every effort by both sides to bring Christians and Muslims closer together and to unify them before the formidable forces of irreligion and secularism, which wield inordinate power today, must be supported by people of faith in both worlds." Organized by a former staffer from the evangelical Youth With a

---

[269] Kevin D. Miller, "Missions' Wild Olive Branch," *Christianity Today*, 9 December 1996, 41.

[270] Steve Rabey, "Mission-Minded Design Strategy for the Muslim World," *Christianity Today* 5 February 1996.

Mission, the goal of the "Reconciliation Walk" was to reach Jerusalem in July 1999, exactly nine centuries after the Crusader invasion.[271]

Sojourners & World Magazines

Conflict defined the nature of the articles related to Muslim-Christians relations during 1996 in *Sojourners*. The religious aspects of the conflict in Bosnia received the most coverage, with one article offering the perspective that "It's not always possible for ordinary Christians to influence international politics, but we can offer to work alongside ordinary Bosnians to help them lay the foundation of a just peace."[272] Muslim-Christian conflict in East Timor was also dealt with in a book review. Additionally, President Clinton was complimented in an article on his attempts to broker peace agreements in the Middle East.[273]

In *World*, Bosnia and the Middle East received a great deal of attention during 1996. The articles in this publication had a much more overtly political focus. In one example, President Clinton and his administration were criticized in a number of articles, including the accusation that Clinton misled Congress about Iranian arms shipments to Bosnian Muslims.[274]

---

[271] Rusty Wright, "Christians Retrace Crusader's Steps," *Christianity Today*, 7 October 1996, 90.

[272] Rose Marie Berger, "Calm Before the Storm?" *Sojourners Magazine*, September-October 1996, 14.

[273] Marie Dennis, "Tunnel Vision: How Netanyahu Undercuts the Peace Process," *Sojourners Magazine*, November-December 1996, 11-12.

[274] "Publick Occurances," *World Magazine*, 28 December 1996.

1997: Christians Under the Gun

Total Articles: 16

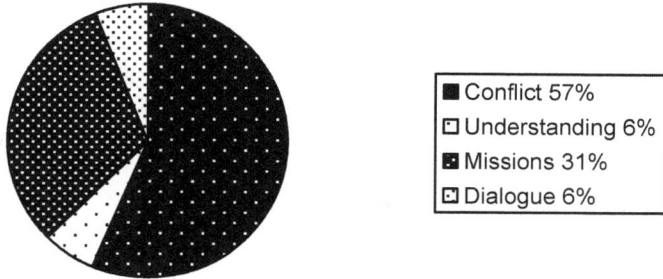

Conflict: 9 Understanding: 1 Missions/Evangelism: 5 Dialogue: 1

Conflict

Conflict articles in 1997 dealt less with informing evangelical readers about core issues of Christian persecution around the world in the manner of Kim Lawton's 1996 expose. Rather, the nine conflict articles primarily came in the form of news reports about instances of Muslim-Christian conflict around the world. This included the Philippines, Egypt (against Coptic Christians), Indonesia, Jerusalem, Pakistan, and Saudi Arabia. The nature of the conflict ranged from mob violence in Indonesia to the beheadings of two Filipino Christians in Saudi Arabia for the crime of armed robbery. (They were noted in the article as leading Christian prayers and Bible studies in the Saudi prison.)[275]

---

[275] Barbara G. Baker, "Two Filipino Christians Beheaded," *Christianity Today*, 1 September 1997, 86.

Understanding

The single item in Christianity Today fitting the category of understanding was a forty-seven word news brief on the New York City Board of Education's decision to settle a suit that would allow the display of the Islamic star and crescent in public schools in conjunction with Christmas displays.[276]

Missions/Evangelism

Hussein Qambar Ali made another appearance in the missions/evangelism category in the pages of *Christianity Today* this year. This time it was about Arab press reports that said he had returned to Islam. However, the article, picked up from the Compass Direct news service, says the organizations cited in the Arab press had no knowledge of the Kuwaiti man's re-conversion. The article also says Ali had married a Christian American woman while in hiding in the United States.[277] Another article later that year deals with the launch of the satellite broadcast of Middle East Television, an evangelism-oriented station based in Lebanon and owned by Pat Robertson.[278]

Pat Robertson's organization Operation Blessing was cited in a short article (202 words) as experiencing a split in management. Dr. Paul R. Williams led a group of former OBI employees to form a new medical missions effort to Muslim-dominated areas in the developing world.[279]

A February article summarized the effort at a missions conference held by InterVarsity Christian Fellowship to "de-Westernize" the

---

[276] "News Briefs," *Christianity Today*, 1 September 1997, 95.

[277] Baker, "Arab Press Says Hussein Has Returned to Islam," *Christianity Today*, 7 April 1997, 56.

[278] Sean Aaron, "CBN Inaugurates Satellite Broadcasts," *Christianity Today*, 6 October 1997, 89.

[279] "Operation Blessing Employees Take Off," *Christianity Today*, 28 April 1997, 85.

gospel in order to be more effective in evangelization. Some attending the conference said that many Muslims living in the developing world associate Christianity with the West, and the West with "sex obsession, drinking, drugs, and family breakdown." Conference participants said missionaries should try to decouple Western cultural trappings from Christian spiritual principles, "allowing them to develop their own distinctive kind of Christianity."[280]

Expanding on this theme was an article by CT Executive Editor David Neff, who wrote of West African converts to Christianity who have not adopted Western worship styles. Neff reported that the Southern Baptist missions board was conducting an experiment in which converts would retain certain practices common in Islamic worship, such as kneeling on prayer mats and chanting scripture, but replaced the Islamic and Quranic worship elements with Christian and Biblical content. Recognizing that some practices are controversial, such as moving the day of worship from Sunday to Friday, Neff says missiologists are watching these experiments closely to see if they lead to higher conversion and retention rates.[281]

Dialogue

In 1997, dialogue did not occupy the focus of a full article in CT, but received mention in a roughly 200-word story about efforts by the National Council of Churches to reach beyond the organization's boundaries for speakers at its general assembly. The article briefly mentions a speech by Imam Warith Deen Mohammad in an article dealing mostly with an address by the head of the National Association of Evangelicals to the NCC.

---

[280] Ted Olsen, "Mission Leaders Seek to De-Westernize Gospel," *Christianity Today*, 3 February 1997, 86.

[281] David Neff, "Going to the Prayer Mat for Jesus," *Christianity Today*, 19 May 1997, 4.

Sojourners and World Magazines

Sojourners coverage took a particularly interfaith/ecumenical turn during 1997. In one article, the author describes traveling among Jews, Christians and Muslims in the Middle East, and exhorting the reader to "become multilingual, at least in the sense that we listen to and respect all the voices. We need to hear the cries for justice—and the petitions and praises to God—in whatever language and posture they are offered."[282]

Another article was a first-person account of a meeting where local Muslim and Christian leaders in Cairo discussed common concerns about the threat of Western culture. The article's author says she realized during the meeting that for most Western Christians, "it is extremely difficult to love people who we treat as invisible or ignore until the next terrorist bombing or overseas scuffle over oil."[283]

In *World*, Bosnia and the continuing role of the American military received significant attention, including, for example, an article critical of the Clinton administration's claim going into the conflict that American troops would be out of the country in one year.[284] Palestinian suicide bombers and tensions in the Middle East also received significant coverage in *World* during 1997.

---

[282] Joyce Hollyday, "Fire, Wind and Water," *Sojourners Magazine*, November-December 1997, 28-32.

[283] Julie Polter, "A Place Apart," *Sojourners Magazine*, May-June 1997, 28-32.

[284] Mindy Belz, "How Much Longer?" *World Magazine*, 13 Dec 1997.

1998: Victory in Congress

Total Articles: 22

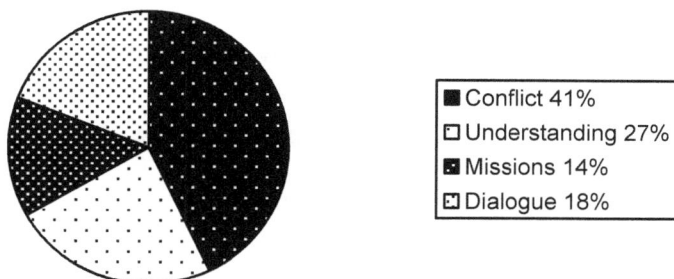

| ■ Conflict 41% |
| □ Understanding 27% |
| ▣ Missions 14% |
| ▣ Dialogue 18% |

Conflict: 9   Understanding: 5 Missions/Evangelism: 3 Dialogue: 4

Conflict

One country, Pakistan, was represented in three of the nine conflict articles appearing in 1998. A December article reported on a Pakistani constitutional amendment allowing the full implementation of Shariah. The amendment, proposed by Prime Minister Nawaz Sharif, was opposed by some in the country under fears that it would create an Islamic regime similar to the Taliban's in neighboring Afghanistan. Shariah-based blasphemy laws were cited as a means of persecuting Christians, with more than 100 Christians charged for the crime "which requires the death penalty for insults to Muhammad."[285]

The other two Pakistan items include a roughly 200-word article on riots stirred by the suicide of Roman Catholic bishop John Joseph. The bishop's suicide was reportedly in protest of the death sentence handed by an Islamic court to a fellow Catholic, Ayub Masih, facing charges of slandering Islam. The court suspended Masih's death

---

[285] "Islamic Law Proposal Raises Tensions," *Christianity Today,* 7 December 1998, 22.

sentence six days after the bishop's suicide. The incidents sparked protests against the blasphemy laws by thousands of Pakistani Christians. Two days after the protest, the article says a "mob of Muslim extremists burned homes and shops in Faisalabad ... in reaction to the protests by the Christian community."[286] A few weeks earlier, CT also published a short news brief on a United Presbyterian Church pastor who was stabbed to death in Sultanpura, Pakistan, and the murder charges against a local Muslim leader.[287]

Other instances of conflict and persecution appearing in CT in 1998 include the jailing and deportation of expatriate Christians in Saudi Arabia, a ban on certain Christian religious activities in Uzbekistan, and a substantial article on Muslim-Christian conflict in Sudan. Another article dealt with the reaction by local Christians to the embassy bombings in Kenya and Tanzania, which tied in local instances of clashes between Muslims and Christians in Kenya.

In March 1998, a 200-word article appeared on the efforts of northern Nigerian Muslim leaders to shut down evangelistic broadcasts sponsored by the Christian Broadcasting Network.[288] Another article reports on an investigation led by Brother Andrew's organization Open Doors, which disputed assertions by the Israeli government and Christian Zionist organizations that the Arab Christian community in the Palestinian territories was suffering extreme harassment and intimidation by "Muslim extremists" and the Palestinian Authority. The Open Doors investigation reportedly found that Palestinian Christian suffered some discrimination, but not the life-threatening persecution that had been purported by some Christian groups.[289]

---

[286] "Persecution: Pakistani Bishop's Death Sparks Riots," *Christianity Today*, 15 June 1998, 18.

[287] "News Briefs," *Christianity Today*, 6 April 1998, 27.

[288] Obed Minchakpu, "Nigeria: Muslims Aim to End Televangelism," *Christianity Today*, 2 March 1998, 78.

[289] Peri Stone, "Persecution Propaganda?" *Christianity Today*, 13 July 1998, 14.

Also an article appearing May 18 reported on the first International Conference on Religious Persecution. The thrust of the conference was to encourage evangelicals to put pressure on the U.S. government to crack down on religious persecution abroad, with the rising Muslim-Christian tension in Nigeria cited as a prime example.[290]

Religious Persecution Bills in Congress

Though the articles do not explicitly falls into the categories involving Muslim-Christian encounters, *Christianity Today* also covered the successful passage on October 9 of the International Religious Freedom Act (IRFA). Upon President Clinton's signing of the bill, an ambassador-at-large on religious persecution was created at the State Department as well as a bipartisan, ten-member commission examining the issue. The commission was charged with producing an annual country-by-country report on religious conflicts worldwide.[291] Before it passed both houses of Congress, IRFA was combined with a competing religious persecution bill. The competing bill, called the "Freedom From Religious Persecution Act," required sanctions against countries guilty of severe religious persecution, an element advocates sought to strengthen in IRFA.[292]

---

[290] Mary Cagney, "Evangelicals Warned Against Persecution Apathy," *Christianity Today*, 18 May 1998, 20.

[291] Christine J. Gardner, "Congress Approves Modified Religious Persecution Bill," *Christianity Today*, 16 November 16, 1998, 32.

[292] Ratliff, "Persecution Bills: Congress May Merge Efforts," *Christianity Today*, 7 September 1998, 27.

Understanding

Five articles fit the category of understanding in 1998. Highlights among these articles include a substantial piece by Bishara Awad, described as a leader among the evangelical churches in Jerusalem and Bethlehem. His article, "Squeezed between Warring Majorities," deals with the stresses placed on the Arab Christian community in the struggle over Israel and the Palestinian territories.[293]

In another article, a Kenyan author wrote about the struggle for democracy, and the push to involve Christians in the political process. It deals in part with the challenge Christians face in the large Muslim population in sub-Saharan Africa. The author, David M. Kasali, says Islam is very appealing to some in Africa because "Muslims come with money from the East" to build fine hospitals and schools and provide loans to people who want to build businesses.[294]

Other articles fitting the understanding category include a book excerpt from Brother Andrew about the relationship between Arab Christians and Muslims in the Middle East. The excerpt did not have a specific focus on conversion. Another article from April highlights an evangelical seminary in Jordan, one of more than a dozen in Muslim countries of the Middle East. Continuing in this theme, a July column by Philip Yancey offers the popular evangelical author's perspective on the difficulties faced by Christians living in the Middle East.

Missions/Evangelism

The most significant article on the effort to convert Muslims to Christianity came in October of this year. The article by Wendy Murray Zoba profiles the evangelistic efforts by Brother Andrew among Arab

---

[293] David M. Kasali, "Squeezed Between Warring Majorities," *Christianity Today*, 16 November 1998, 68.

[294] David M. Kasali, "Cursed By Superficiality," *Christianity Today*, 16 November 1998, 56.

Muslims. Zoba characterizes the challenge of Islam as primarily theological: "Brother Andrew says that Islam threatens the viability of Christianity in this region and internationally, not because these nations have oil (integral though that may be in this picture), but because Islam has forced the question *Who is God?* And Western evangelicals have been unable to answer that question."

Zoba quotes Andrew as seeing the evangelical relationship with Muslims as "a very difficult time of total misunderstanding, miscommunication, misinformation, hostility, and not talking to each other." She quotes Andrew as saying Christians need to exercise the same degree of interest in the well-being of Muslims, and the same courage to try improving the lives of those living in the Middle East, that Christians showed behind the Iron Curtain during the Cold War. In addition to holding meetings to encourage solidarity among Arab Christian churches, Andrew is cited as having meetings with members of Hamas and Hizbollah to discuss his goals for social action as well as to "witness boldly about Jesus."[295] (Four years before this article was written, Brother Andrew described his efforts to dodge Israeli controls to bring medical supplies to Hamas members, pray with Muslims, and discuss the role of *Isa* in Islam and Christianity.)[296]

Other missions and evangelism articles were short news items. One was about the launch of the first full-time radio broadcasts by the Far East Broadcasting Company in Indonesia. The other was an article about a "non-traditional" revival in Egypt by evangelist Luis Palau. Palau's videotaped sermon was played simultaneously in hundreds of Presbyterian churches around Egypt. High interest in the message prompted some Protestant churches to hold overflow screenings of Palau's sermon in larger Coptic and Catholic churches.[297]

---

[295] Wendy Murray Zoba, "Brother Andrew's Boldest Mission Yet: 'Smuggling' Jesus Into Muslim Hearts," *Christianity Today,* 5 October 1998, 50.

[296] Brother Andrew, interview with author, July 1994, Hilversum, The Netherlands.

[297] Patricia C. Roberts, "Crowds Exceed Palau's Expectations," *Christianity Today,* 27 April 1998, 22.

Dialogue

Three articles fit the category of dialogue in 1998. The longest was written by an anonymous Christian in an unnamed "Southcentral Asian country" discussing the place of Jesus in Christianity, Islam and Hinduism as he grew up in the milieu of all three religions. The author speaks of the reverence for Jesus among Muslims and the similarities between biblical and Quranic accounts of his birth and life.[298]

Another article discusses the cooperation of Christians, Muslims and Hindus in the effort to secure democracy in Guyana. As tensions rose among different ethnic faction in the drafting the South American country's constitution, the Guyana Council of Churches is cited as cosponsoring a national prayer service with Hindu and Muslim leaders. Another example of cooperation and discussion between Muslims and Christians was cited in the common protest of a museum exhibit in Auckland New Zealand entitled *Virgin in a Condom*. The author notes that another exhibit that featured a female, bare-chested Jesus in *The Last Supper* prompted "outrage" by Catholics, Protestants and Muslims alike.[299]

Sojourners and World Magazines

In its November-December issue for 1998, *Sojourners* responded to the attacks against the U.S. embassies in Kenya and Tanzania by openly promoting dialogue and understanding among American Christians toward American Muslims, in addition to urging the U.S. government to have a more even-handed approach to foreign policy in the Middle East. A commentary by Jim Wallis underscored the connection between local understanding and international conflict: "Because the basis of this terrorism is understood as more theological than ideological, it poses the real danger of a confrontation between the

---

[298] Anonymous, "Stripping Jesus of His Western Garb," *Christianity Today*, 16 November 1998, 65.

[299] Vic Francis, "Virgin in a Condom Provokes Outcry," *Christianity Today*, 15 June 1998, 19.

primarily Christian West and Islamic fundamentalism. There is profound misunderstanding between Christians and Muslims, which underlines the potential for conflict, even though the mainstream of each religion does not want it."[300]

Another *Sojourners* article points out that theologically-conservative Christians do not need to give up their core beliefs to cooperate with, and better understand, their Muslim neighbors: "While Christians and Muslims will not come to complete theological agreement (with one another or among themselves), we can come to a better mutual understanding. And, by living out the best of our religious traditions, we can 'compete with one another in good works."[301]

In *World*, the emphasis on news items and articles dealing with Muslims or contact between Muslims and Christians continued the theme of persecution and conflict. In the same time period that *Sojourners* was promoting dialogue and understanding, *World* was reminding readers of the difficulties Christians suffered in Muslim countries such as Sudan and Indonesia, in addition to non-Muslims areas such as China and Southeast Asia.[302] The magazine reported the progress of the "Freedom From Religious Persecution Act," saying that: "it was not clear whether President Clinton would sign the measure. The administration has persistently sided with big business in frowning on any legislation that links trade with human rights."[303]

---

[300] Jim Wallis, "A Better Way to Fight Terrorism," *Sojourners Magazine*, November-December 1998, 9-10.

[301] Charles Kimball, "Is Islam the Enemy?" *Sojourners Magazine*, November-December 1998, 16-21. Surah 5:48.

[302] "Persecution Goes Global: Over time, Only the Names Have Changed," *World Magazine* 28 November 1998.

[303] "Publick Occurrences: The Week," *World Magazine,* 24 October 1998.

1999: Rise in Dialogue

Total Articles: 22

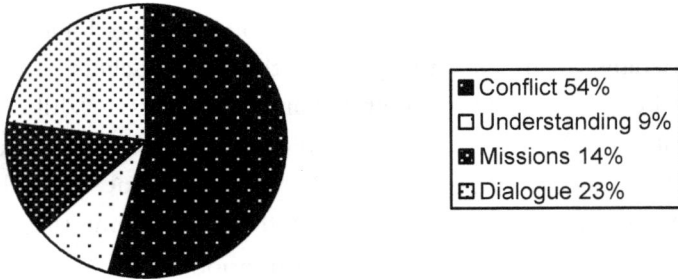

Conflict: 12   Understanding: 2 Missions/Evangelism: 3 Dialogue: 5

Conflict

An August 9 CT editorial begins with the sentence: "Thanks largely to the efforts of Michael Horowitz, a Jew, the 1990's will likely be remembered as the era when evangelicals became aware of the persecution of our Christian brothers and sisters in Sudan, China and elsewhere."[304] The editorial does not elaborate further on Horowitz, but rather points out that the rise in evangelical interest in the persecution of Christians around the world has led to the formation, in 1998, of the U.S. Commission on International Freedom and the appointment of a State Department ambassador to monitor religious persecution around the world. This editorial shows a solidification of the idea that evangelicals should identify closely with Christian victims of persecution overseas. This article extends the idea that evangelicals should look after fellow Christians, even if they may follow another

---

[304] "Persecution is Persecution is Persecution," *Christianity Today*, 9 August 1999, 27.

stream of Christianity, in addition to those of other faiths including Hindus, Buddhists and Muslims.[305]

Other articles in the conflict category continue to reinforce the concept of the worldwide persecuted church by pointing out oppressive laws, such as those against "blasphemy" in Pakistan.[306] Rioting connected to both ethnic and religious tensions in, for example, Nigeria and Indonesia also was reported by CT in 1999.[307]

Understanding

There were two articles in the category of understanding in 1999, appearing in May and June of that year. The shorter May article dealt with the international churches in Kuwait, where many from non-Muslim Arab countries attend services in many different languages.[308] The June article is perhaps the more significant in both its size and subject matter. Ajith Fernando, an author and national director of Youth for Christ in Sri Lanka sought to inform American evangelicals that, while they may identify with Christians around the world, Christians (including evangelicals) in the developing world often identify American Christians with Western culture, American military power, and memories of colonialism. An example Ajith points out was the appearance of Billy Graham with President George H.W. Bush on the first day of the Gulf War, which unsettled some in his community. Ajith cautions Western Christians against using buzzwords that deal

---

[305] Ibid.

[306] Ethan Casey, "Pakistan's Despised Christians," *Christianity Today*, 26 April 1999, 94.

[307] "In brief," *Christianity Today*, 15 November 1999, 29.

[308] Grace Pundyk, "Kuwait's Desert Oasis: A Church With 42 Nationalities," *Christianity Today*, 24 May 1999, 22.

with "defeating strongholds and the forces of evil," encouraging them instead adopt a discourse emphasizing love and sacrifice.[309]

Missions/Evangelism

Among the three articles falling into this category is a news brief on the limits of Christian relief efforts in Iraq toward members of the country's churches suffering under U.N. sanctions. Another deals with the outflow of missionaries from Filipino churches to countries that are sometimes hostile to Christian activity, such as Saudi Arabia.[310]

But the most significant article dealing with missionary efforts among Muslims by evangelicals is an editorial dealing with religious freedom and the right to convert. As evangelicals, believing strongly in a biblical mandate to spread the Gospel, the article proposes using the newfound powers stemming from the International Religious Freedom Act to pressure countries to loosen laws that make it illegal to change religions. The article cites Egyptian law preventing a convert to Christianity from changing his official papers, in addition to examples of governmental religious preferences to certain religions in countries ranging from India to Chile.[311]

Dialogue

The "Reconciliation Walk" intended to heal cultural wounds between Muslims and Christians caused by the Crusades 900 years ago makes another appearance in the dialogue category this year.[312] The

---

[309] Ajith Fernando, "Bombs Away: How Western Military Actions Affect the Work of the Church," *Christianty Today,* 14 June 1999, 76.

[310] "Missionaries in Harm's Way," *Christianity Today,* 14 June 1999, 19.

[311] "Protecting the Right to Convert," *Christianity Today,* 1 March 1999, 28.

[312] Tomas Dixon, "Reconciliation Walk: Apology Crusaders to Enter Israel," *Christianity Today,* 5 April 1999, 23.

brief April 5 article previews the targeted July date when the Christians enter Israel on the anniversary of the Crusader invasion of Jerusalem.

This article was followed up in the September issue recounting the entry of "450 American and European Christians, most of them evangelicals, gathering in Jerusalem to ask forgiveness for the historical bloodshed and for a lingering 'crusader mentality' in the church today."[313] Rabbi Lau of the Great Synagogue in Jerusalem is quoted in the article as telling participants that Jews have been praying for the victims of the Crusades for nine centuries, and that "you came very late, but better late than never."[314] Though positive interactions with Muslims were reported, no Muslims were quoted in the article.

One short news item dealt with Turkish churches coordinating earthquake aid in the Izmit region. It said there were about 3,500 evangelicals living in the Muslim country. The article says that in the past Muslim officials resisted church activities such as establishing church camps, but welcomed efforts after the quake to establish tent cities for those left homeless as well as the distribution of food and clothing.[315]

Another article deals with ethnic and religious strife in Nigeria, and the desire among some Muslims and Christians to develop relationships and dialogue to ease some of those tensions. The article points to a history of violence and rivalry in Nigeria, and the pressures Christians face in the Muslim-dominated northern states. It said leaders from both religions recognize that violence between Muslims and Christians has the potential to "Balkanize" Nigeria, and endanger the

313 _____. "An Apology, 900 Years in the Making," *Christianity Today*, 6 September 1999, 2.
314 Ibid.
315 Jody Veenker, "Churches Coordinate Earthquake Aid," *Christianity Today*, 4 October 1999, 22a.

stabilizing effect the most-populous African nation has in West Africa.[316]

Billy Graham's meeting with Iraqi Chaldean Patriarch Raphael Bidawad and Ayatollah Sayyid al-Sadr was the focus of a 200-word news item in this year. The goodwill gesture by the Iraqi Christian and Muslim leaders was designed to raise awareness about a UNICEF report on how sanctions against Saddam Hussein's regime were contributing to the deaths of thousands of children in the country. The article says Graham was invited to go to Iraq, but the aging evangelist suggested that his son, Franklin, go as a representative of Samaritan's Purse to seek ways to provide relief to suffering Iraqis.[317]

Sojourners and World Magazines

In 1999, *Sojourners* dealt mostly with the conflict in the Balkans. The magazine reported numerous positive encounters between Muslims and Christians. One article titled "A Laboratory of Reconciliation," dealt with efforts to rebuild bridges between ethnic Muslims and Christians in the former Yugoslavia.[318] Another article highlighted the work of evangelical Albanians in aiding Muslim refugees, providing food and clothing. The article's author was Dr. Clive Calver, president of World Relief, an evangelical NGO. Calver writes: "I asked one of the Muslim refugee families, 'How do you feel about these so-called Christians [Serbian militants] who forced you out of your homes?' A young man adjacent to us abruptly broke in and

---

[316] Steve Chambers, "Can Christianity and Islam Coexist and Prosper?" *Christianity Today*, 25 October 1999, 22.

[317] "Graham Meets With Iraqi Leaders," *Christianity Today*, 15 November 1999, 15.

[318] Rose Marie Berger, "A Laboratory of Reconciliation," *Sojourners Magazine*, November-December 1999, 24.

answered, "But they aren't Christians. The people here caring for us are real Christians."[319]

In *World*, evangelical NGO's were also noted for providing aid in Kosovo in an article that concentrated mostly on NATO airstrikes against Serbs.[320] The events in Kosovo were followed closely in *World*, with attention also given to hot spots for Muslim-Christian conflict such as Sudan and Pakistan. Notable among the news items in this year was a report that a conservative Muslim newspaper in Turkey, *Zaman*, criticized the Turkish government for a raid on a Protestant church in the port city of Izmir. The short, 138-word article mentions criticism coming from a number of Turkish publications saying that "the apparent 'crime' [in the raid] was to be both a Turk and a Christian."[321] World Relief's Clive Calver also makes an appearance in *World's* coverage of evangelical relief efforts in Turkey during the aftermath of a severe earthquake.[322]

---

[319] Clive Calver, "We've Got To Give Them Back Their Hope," *Sojourners Magazine*, July August 1999, 29.

[320] "Publick Occurrences Both Foreign and Domestick," *World Magazine*, 3 April 1999.

[321] "Publick Occurrences Both Foreign and Domestick," *World Magazine*, 9 October 1999.

[322] Mindy Belz, "A Christian Opportunity?" *World Magazine*, 11 September 1999.

2000: Rise in Bloodshed

Total Articles: 28

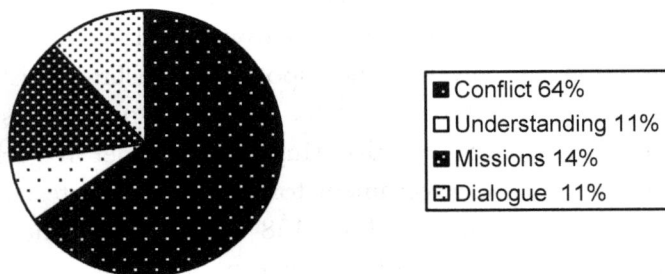

Conflict: 17   Understanding: 2 Missions/Evangelism: 4 Dialogue: 3

Conflict

Muslim–Christian riots in Indonesia and Nigeria typified the conflict articles in this year. The uprisings in these two countries left thousands dead, and threatened to create an unending cycle of attacks and retaliation. In Indonesia, Christians complained that the Muslim-dominated government failed to fully suppress the slaughter of Christian civilians.[323] One article reported Indonesian naval ships blockaded two islands 1,600 miles northeast of Jakarta in order to prevent more Muslims from pouring into the area, and to keep the violence from spreading. The blockade prompted a demonstration in Jakarta by 90,000 Muslims "demanding a holy war against Christians."[324]

Five articles dealt with the adoption of Shariah into the civil code of Northern Nigerian states, and the ensuing riots that left thousands

---

[323] "Christians and Muslims Still Fighting, Dying in Ambon," *Christianity Today*, 13 November 2000.

[324] "2,000 Die in Muslim-Christian Conflict," *Christianity Today*, 7 February 2000, 32.

dead and tens of thousands homeless. As Christian organizations under the umbrella of the Christian Association of Nigeria (CAN) battled the implementation of Shariah in Nigeria's courts, riots broke out in cities with large populations of both Muslims and Christians.[325]

In February 2000, Muslim rioters destroyed the Baptist Theological Seminary in Kaduna, killing three students and two staff during a massive riot that killed hundreds, prompting retaliations from the Christian community.[326] Muslim-dominated Nigerian states spanning the northern part of the country adopted Shariah during the first year after Nigeria held democratic elections, during which they installed a president who was a self-declared Baptist.[327]

Also this year, 20 Coptic Christians and one Muslim were killed in a January shootout that included women, children and teenagers. The al-Kosheh skirmish reportedly broke out as the result of a dispute between a Christian merchant and a Muslim customer. One article outlines how tensions have risen between Muslims and Christians in the town since 1998, when similar riots broke out over rumors that a Muslim family killed two Christians (who were actually killed in a gambling brawl).[328] In the search for the murderer, hundreds of Christians were rounded up and experienced "often brutal" interrogations by the local police.[329]

The February article says the Christian community stoked anger among the local Muslims after the August 1998 riots because the incident garnered so much international sympathy for the Christian community. The story reported that the al-Kosheh Christians became emboldened to the point they ignored Egyptian laws against rebuilding

---

[325] "Churches Challenge Islamic Law," *Christianity Today*, 4 September 2000.

[326] "Briefs: The World," *Christianity Today*, 12 June 2000, 27.

[327] Obed Minchakpu, "Islamic law Raises Tensions," *Christianity Today*, 10 January 2000, 26.

[328] Kees Hulsman, "20 Coptic Christians Die as Village Tensions Rise," *Christianity Today*, 7 February 2000, 31.

[329] Ibid.

churches, and began openly confronting the Egyptian government with human-rights violations. One Egyptian journalist is noted for saying that the newly found "arrogance" of the Christians made Muslims feel the demand to "knock them down hard."[330]

Understanding

Of note in this category is a February article describing "thousands" of Christians and Muslims flooding Nativity Square in Bethlehem to greet the orthodox Patriarchs of Constantinople and Jerusalem. The article describes the stresses Orthodox churches are facing in the Middle East with the emigration of Arab Christians to the West, and complaints from lay members of the church that want more religious support from the Orthodox hierarchy.[331]

Missions/Evangelism

Evangelistic activity both in the United States and abroad appear in this category during 2000. An April issue featured a cover story on the "threat" of Islam among African-American Christians in the U.S., and attempts to reconvert and stave off the religion's influence.[332] An example of global missions and evangelism in CT coverage during 2000 is an article on the work of the Salvation Army in Chechnya, providing medical care and rehabilitation for Muslim children suffering from war wounds in the fight between rebels and the Russian government.[333]

---

[330] Ibid.

[331] Elaine Ruth Fletcher, "Orthodox Leaders Closer to Unity," *Christianity Today*, 7 February 2000, 30.

[332] Edward Gilbreath, "How Islam is Winning Black America," *Christianity Today*, 3 April 2000, 52.

[333] Beverly Nickels, "Saving Bodies, Rescuing Souls," *Christianity Today*, 24 April 2000, 28.

Dialogue

Most significant dialogue writing in 2000 was a three-part series on Islam written by Wendy Murray Zoba, anchored in the same issue as the missions/evangelism story on African-Americans and Islam. The author, an associate editor of CT, endeavored to educate readers about Islamic theology as it compares to Christianity, as well as encourage evangelicals to learn more about Muslim beliefs and culture. Zoba writes that, alongside efforts to present the Christian gospel, Christians are challenged to learn more about Muslims living in the United States and make friends with them. The article in the print version of the story was expanded into a much fuller Internet presentation on steps to understanding and dialogue between Muslims and Christians.[334]

Sojourners and World Magazines

Sojourners articles in this subject area moved away from the ecumenism and dialogue of the previous years, with conflict-centered articles on areas such as Sudan. The most significant article was by Ryan Beiler, who described his impressions of the difficult work undertaken by a Mennonite organization in Uganda to provide relief for Sudanese refugees fleeing battles between Muslims and Christians in that country.[335]

World's coverage in 2000 included articles on the persecution of Muslim converts to Christianity in Iran and Yemen, and the "bureaucratic hostility" these converts faced when appealing to Western government and the UNHCR for help. In the midst of conflict-focused articles, one *World* editorial called for increased

---

[334] Wendy Murray Zoba, "Engaging Our Muslim Neighbors," *Christianity Today*, 3 April 2000, 40.

[335] Ryan Beiler, "Spectacular Works, Simple Obedience," *Sojourners Magazine*, September-October, 36.

religious pluralism in the American public square. The subject of the article was the nomination by Republican House Speaker Dennis Hastert (an evangelical) of a Roman Catholic chaplain for the House of Representatives. The author advocated wider religious representation in official roles in American government: "The United States is not a Jewish state or a Catholic state; not a Protestant state or Muslim state. And it certainly should not be a secularized state."[336]

Framing the Challenge of Islam

The articles appearing in *Christianity Today* and similar publications show some of the same characteristics as a social movement organization within Benford and Snow's system for analyzing the formation of ideas and actions.[337] However, evangelicalism, at least as it is examined through broadly-targeted press coverage, is best regarded as a "sentiment pool" or "preference cluster" according to Benford and Snow's theory.

In the case of "frame bridging" and conflict, the editors of CT, *World* and *Sojourners* are employing the use of mass media, including printed magazines and the Internet, to introduce and reinforce the idea that Christians are a persecuted people and evangelicals should feel connected to those are suffering religious oppression. From a proselytization standpoint, evangelicals may often regard indigenous Christians in developing countries as merely nominal or even outside of the faith.[338] However, when it comes to garnering support to form U.S. policy advancing religious freedom, those same Christians are often portrayed as fellow believers suffering at the hands, primarily, of Muslims.

---

[336] James W. Skillen, "Judgment Calls: Genuine Pluralism," *World Magazine*, 7 October 2000.

[337] Benford and Snow, "Frame Alignment Processes," 467-472.

[338] Damian Efta, "Who are the Unreached?" 1.

The articles cited here also demonstrate that those in activist or editorial roles amplified certain values, such as solidarity with fellow Christians and a need for constructive relationships with them. This in turn made Muslim-Christian encounters on the global scene a pressing issue for American evangelicals. In the pages of CT and other evangelical magazines, the reader finds repeated instances of rioting and violence between Muslims and Christians – with Muslims portrayed the primary perpetrators. In doing so they have employed "frame extension" of situations and concerns that at first glance may have little direct bearing on the daily lives theologically-conservative American Protestants, but given the movement's political clout, have a great influence on efforts to shape U.S. policy (i.e. the International Religious Freedom Act).

As the framing of conflict appears as the primary form of encounter between Muslims and Christians, dialogue emerges as playing a minor but important role. For example, Brother Andrew appears in some articles as an agent of proselytization. However, he also appears in "dialogue" articles as an evangelical who builds relationships with Palestinian Muslims that go beyond efforts to convert. His work takes place through contacts that offer religious and cultural understanding as well as an effort to meet physical needs. The "Reconciliation Walk" from 1996 to 1999 that retraced the steps of the Crusaders shows another attempt to form a foundation of cooperation and positive relationships between Muslims and Christians.

With the attention of evangelicals on the persecution of Christians in the Muslim world, the terrain became somewhat less amenable to interfaith understanding and between Muslims and Christians. However, for some activists such as Brother Andrew, engagement with the Other seemed to cultivate an perspective that allowed for a constructive relationship with certain Muslim groups.

Beginning in 1996, and continuing through 2000, the thunder of conflict filled the pages of the evangelical press, with distant but distinct flashes of dialogue. For evangelicals tending a crop of new ideas and responses to fresh challenges, Muslims and the religion of

Islam remained clouds on the horizon, portending a storm. The next chapter will deal with the flurry of debate over the cultural fallout from the Sept. 11 attacks among periodicals in the evangelical family.

7

MUSLIM ENCOUNTERS IN THE EVANGELICAL PRESS: 2001 TO 2003

In the pages of *Christianity Today* and other publications, Christian persecution at the hands of Muslims was used as a means to extend the evangelical's sense of connection to those Christians of many varieties who suffered abroad. In a manner true to modern evangelicalism's effort to remain engaged with the wider culture, this "frame extension" drew evangelicals into the debate over religious freedom on the international scene.

This engagement resulted in evangelicals becoming a powerful voice in U.S. foreign policy, in addition to the political weight they carried in domestic politics. It also created a cultural terrain in which evangelicals could easily view Muslims and the religion of Islam as a threat.

The shock of the Sept. 11th attacks transformed the challenge of Islam and Muslims from the international to the domestic scene. Just as the arrival of modernism in the previous century had posed a theological challenge to evangelicalism, the Sept.11th attacks forced evangelicals to consider the nature of their engagement with Muslims apart from the mission field. The pages of the evangelical publications show a community looking for a way ahead as it roiled with anger, confusion, and the same sense of loss that many Americans felt. This chapter takes a look at these reactions, and how they evolved into distinct evangelical approaches toward the challenge of Islam and Muslims.

The previous chapter focused on four categories (conflict, understanding/context, missions/evangelism, and dialogue) as they appeared in *Christianity Today* in the years before 2001, and included a quick survey of two other publications falling on either side of the political spectrum. This chapter will also examine the same landscape and look at the same features. However, it will also dial in the magnification on the coverage of the subject through a CT's website, as well as the publications *Sojourners* and *World*.

This chapter will first take a look at 2001 evangelical press coverage before Sept. 11 in the three publications. That overview will be followed by CT's immediate response to the attacks as seen through their Internet coverage. It will then return to the print publications for the remainder of 2001 through 2003. In 2002 there was a flood of material published in CT, *Sojourners* an *World* related to the challenge of Islam and Muslims, so CT coverage of that year will be broken up into quarters to better show the trends at work.

The suddenness and the magnitude Sept. 11 attacks effectively tilled up the soil on the evangelical family farm, laying bare how different segments of this community dealt with theological and cultural tests in a shifting environment.

2001: Shifts in the Cultural Landscape

Total Articles: 30

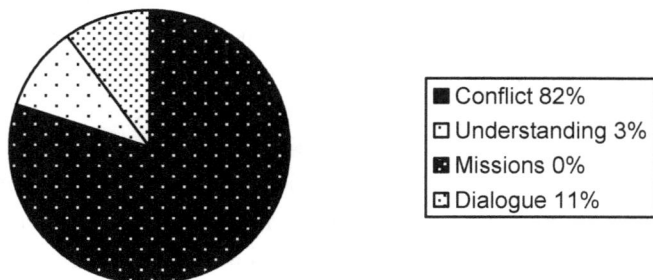

Conflict: 24   Understanding: 3   Missions/Evangelism: 0 Dialogue: 3

January through August:

Conflict:

Sixteen articles fell into the category of conflict in the months leading up to the September 11th attacks. Most documented Muslim-Christian violence in incidents were similar to those in this category in previous years. In January, one article compared the increasing religious violence in Kenya to the ongoing, large-scale confrontation in Nigeria. As in Nigeria, the correspondent reported the tensions were from the desire by northern Muslims to implement Shariah. This article also depicts a priest, standing in the doorway of his church, imploring parishioners that were arming themselves to fight Muslims, "This is craziness; this is stupidity ... This is blasphemous and has nothing to do with God."[339] A prominent Muslim is quoted as blaming the rise in interreligious conflict on the unpopular government, which had been

---

[339] Odhiambo Okite, "Muslim-Christian Riots Rock Nairobi," *Christianity Today*, 8 January 2001, 33.

facing calls for constitutional reform from both Muslims and Christians.[340]

Another conflict article picked up from the Compass Direct news service told of four Christians arrested and detained in Brunei for praying in their home. The indigenous Christians were accused of evangelizing Muslims, participating in "cult" activities and smuggling Indonesian Bibles into the country.[341]

One of the most alarming conflict stories from the pages of *Christianity Today* appeared in May. The author tells the story of a Catholic family that watched as their 14-year-old daughter was kidnapped by seven to ten Muslim men. The story said the family rushed to the house of one of the men they recognized, eventually learning of her fate from his relatives, "[Ahmed] has your daughter, but she is converted to Islam ... Your girl is no longer a virgin."[342]

The story was used by the author as a case-in-point for the numerous instances of the rape of Christian girls by Pakistani Muslim "extremists" wishing to intimidate Christians. In this case, local officials reportedly refused to help the family, but city officials in Lahore, under pressure from an American organization called International Christian Concern, concluded that the alleged conversion and thumb-printed marriage certificate was fake. However, it said the family continues to search for their daughter.[343]

In the same issue of CT, an article appears reported the "cold shoulder" members of the U.S. Commission on International Religious Freedom received during a visit to Egypt. Although the delegation successfully met with the leaders of the country's Coptic community and the head of Al-Azhar University, other Christian and Muslim

---

[340] Ibid.

[341] Jeff Taylor, "Christians in Detention for Prayer," *Christianity Today*, 23 April 2001, 27.

[342] C. Hope Flinchbaugh, "Stolen Daughter," *Christianity Today*, 21 May 2001, 30.

[343] Ibid.

religious refused to meet with them. One bishop was quoted as saying Christians "are capable of finding solutions in Egypt without any foreign intervention." Another human rights activist compared the U.S. government to a bull in a china shop, saying that American pressure for religious rights in Egypt would exacerbate "ill feelings from Muslims, which only can spell trouble for Christians."[344]

Christianity Today also began its reporting of the May 27 kidnapping of Martin and Gracia Burnham in the Philippines. The Abu Sayyaf separatist group abducted the veteran New Tribes Mission missionaries, and threatened to behead the couple if their demands (unspecified in the article) were not met.[345]

The previous chapter demonstrated that the articles appearing in CT rarely crossed the boundary into mobilization of the reader, (thereby keeping the audience in the category of "sentiment pool" rather than a social movement organization).[346] During mid-2001, CT gives the first indication of change in approach toward advocacy in this area. An article on the persecution of Christians in Sudan appeared in the June 11 issue in 2001 outlining specific steps for evangelical readers to influence U.S. government policy with regard to Sudan. The author, Jeff Sellers, tells the reader "a halt to Arab persecution of black Christians (and animists) in southern Sudan first requires a political solution." Sellers then instructs the reader to write Secretary of State Colin Powell, pray for the southern Sudanese, and et rid of shares in companies like Talisman Energy Inc., which do business with Sudan.[347]

---

[344] Kees Hulsman, "Religious Freedom Delegation Gets Cold Shoulder," *Christianity Today*, 21 May 2001, 28.

[345] "Kidnapped Missionaries Reported Safe," *Christianity Today*, 6 August 2001, 28.

[346] David A. Snow, E. Burke Rochford, et al., "Frame Alignment Processes, Micromobilization, and Movement Participation," 464-481.

[347] Jeff M. Sellers, "No Greater Tragedy," 11 June 2001, 95.

Understanding

Two items fell into this category in the eight months leading up to the September 11 attacks. The first was a timeline of conflict in the Holy land, outlining events in the establishment of Israel from 1948 through the present. The article, which pays special attention to the peace process in the 1990's, mentions periods of Jewish, Christian and Muslim rule over the area over the centuries.[348] The other "understanding" article deals with the steady growth experienced within the Muslim community in the United States. The article outlines the findings of a study cosponsored by the Council on American-Islamic Relations (CAIR) and Hartford Seminary. The article, which appears in the same issue as the "conflict" article calling for political action among Christians, cited increased involvement in mosques among American Muslims, and the role of the mosque as a base "for political and social mobilization."[349] The article also cited demographic trends among American citizens who have converted to Islam and those who have emigrated from Muslim countries.

One of the researchers quoted in the article remarked on the recent rise in the number of white converts to Islam: "I don't think this would have been true a few decades ago ... As the horns are taken off Islam and people begin to seriously consider it, Islam becomes more acceptable in the minds of all American people."[350]

Dialogue

Another pair of articles in this year falls under the category of "dialogue." In February, CT published an article on the approval by Britain's House of Lords of "therapeutic" human embryo cloning, despite protests from the United Kingdom's religious communities.

---

[348] "Conflict in the Holy land," 8 January 2001, 68.
[349] "Muslims Report Steady Growth."
[350] Ibid.

The article quotes both Catholic and Protestant leaders opposed to the practice, but it also highlights the cooperation between a number of Muslim, Christian and Jewish leaders in drafting a unified opposition to the impending act of parliament. A letter from the various religious groups opposing human embryo cloning shared signatures from 11 religious leaders, ranging from the Archbishop of Canterbury to the general secretary of the Baptist Union and the president of The Muslim College in London.[351]

The other dialogue article, appearing in the June 11 issue, dealt with an address in Kuala Lumpur by Malaysian Prime Minister Mahatir bin Mohamed to the World Evangelical Fellowship. The prime minister told the gathering that once interreligious violence begins, it can continue for generations. The thrust of Mahatir's speech was to encourage "dialogue and tolerance," while recognizing the fact that "it is the nature of some religious denominations that propagation of their faith is obligatory," Mahatir said in the speech. He added, "But we should be careful that we don't propagate religions at the cost of conflict and violence." The director of the Pentecostal Assemblies of God denomination was reported as saying that the prime minister's presence at the gathering actually helped the Christian community by encouraging its credibility in Malaysia, and gave Christians a "better standing with government when we need to negotiate and get government approval."[352]

Post-September 11th: Response on ChristianityToday.com

The Sept. 11 attacks drew a sizable and thoughtful response from the editors of CT. However, some readers did not see this response until long after the attacks. A common feature of monthly magazine

---

[351] Cedric Pulford, "House of Lords Legalizes Human Embryo Cloning," 5 March 2001, 32.

[352] Anil Stephen, "Muslim Leader Appeals to Evangelicals," *Christianity Today*, 11 June 2001, 24.

publishing is the lag-time that exists between the time an article is written and the date when the periodical hits the shelves. An author can easily wait a month or more to see a freshly written article appear in the pages of the magazine.

To respond quickly to the attacks of September 11, the editors of CT turned to the magazine's website to offer evangelical readers a more immediate perspective on what had happened. During the late 1990's, Christianity Today developed a strong Internet presence, with an ever-growing website that encompasses CT and its sister publications. Although the web articles cannot be categorized as carrying the same reach (and permanency) in the evangelical milieu as those printed in the magazine, they nonetheless offer valuable insight into the immediate thoughts and emotions that shuddered through the evangelical movement in the first days and weeks after the attacks.

One of the first postings on Christianity Today's website was a collection of past CT editorials dealing with the Christian response to feeling of anger, fear and hatred in the wake of tragedy. In the hours after the planes hit the World Trade Center and the Pentagon, the editors wrote, "it is unknown who is behind today's attacks, but it is certain that many Americans are already blaming radical Muslim and Arab groups – and hatred seems to be a common theme on today's call-in programs." The key message in the editorial was, "In times like this, as in all other times, Christians have a responsibility to love above all else."[353]

CT's Internet coverage of the Sept. 11 attacks also included reporting from New York by the magazine's senior news writer, Tony Carnes. An article entitled "In the Belly of the Beast" posted on September 12 typifies the response Carnes observed among evangelical churches near Ground Zero. He wrote that churches near the site of the attacks in New York opened their doors as sanctuaries for those fleeing the site of the World Trade Center. He also reports that Christians organized prayer groups soon after the attacks, and

---

[353] "Fear and Hate," *Christianity Today*, 11 September 2001.

dispatched teams to help those wounded and shaken by the traumatic events. At least one evangelical group sent doctors and nurses to a local hospital.[354]

Edward Gilbreath, associate editor of *Christianity Today*, penned an article posted three days after the attacks addressing the question, "What do we do with all this anger?" He wrote that in the moments that Americans felt the greatest wave of fear and sadness over the loss of life and the violence of the attacks, "we witnessed footage of Middle Eastern exultation. We saw men and women cheering and praising Allah for our misfortune." He wrote, "We saw the enemy, and they were Muslim."[355]

Gilbreath noted instances of anti-Arab and anti-Muslim attacks around the country, including death threats sent to local mosques and bricks thrown through the window of an Islamic bookstore. He said that even "many usually even-tempered Christian men and women are finding it difficult to feel anything but reciprocal wrath for the individuals who engineered and executed the gruesome attacks." Gilbreath suggests one way evangelicals can respond to anti-Arab and anti-Muslim sentiment is to offer emotional support to Arabs and Muslims who may be feeling "alienated within their own communities." He said the challenge for Christians in the wake of the attacks is to respond in a healthy way, asking readers, "ultimately, how do we forgive?"[356]

Despite calls for a sober, healthy response, CT web editor Ted Olsen pointed out a number of missteps by media outlets and public figures. At the top of the list was President Bush's reference to the war on terrorism as a "crusade." Georgetown University's Yvonne Haddad responded in the story, saying the word "crusade" to Muslims is "as

---

[354] Tony Carnes, "In the Belly of the Beast," *Christianity Today*, 12 September 2001.

[355] Edward Gilbreath, "Taking it Personally," *Christianity Today*, 14 September 2001.

[356] Ibid.

bad to their ears as it is when we hear *jihad.*"[357] Olsen also refers to the "Jerry Falwell fiasco," and quotes an atheist who said her atheism has only been strengthened by the events of September 11 and their aftermath. In another example, Olsen points out that Fox News Channel referred viewers during one program to an arm of the Church of Scientology for counseling.

However, Olsen wrote that the "worst mistake on television" belonged to the Dutch Muslim Broadcasting Company (Nederlandse Moslim Omroep), which "immediately after the country's three minutes of silence honoring the victims of the attack, started broadcasting threatening texts from the Quran. One such scripture: 'to those who do not believe: their properties and their children will not conciliate Allah. They are but fuel to the fire." Olsen, taking his information from the Ananova news website, said that the company apologized, calling the broadcast a human error.[358]

In another article, Olsen examined whether "Islam is really a religion of peace." In it he quotes the director of London's Institute for the Study of Islam and Christianity, Patrick Sookhdeo, as saying "There are clearly two strands in contemporary Islam: the peaceable and the war-like. Islam is not one or the other; it is clearly both at the same time."[359]

Ten days after the attacks, the editors of CT began to post articles on their web site that examined the issue of religion and violence, as well as the response of a Christian community searching for both justice and reconciliation. CT managing Editor Mark Galli wrote a piece called "Now What?" in which he asserted that "no religion holds a corner on terrorism," including Islam. Drawing from studies by scholars such as the University of Santa Barbara's Mark Juergensmeyer,

---

[357] Ted Olsen, "Weblog: Attack Brings Out the Best and Worst of Public Religion," *Christianity Today*, 19 September 2001.

[358] "Dutch TV Company Broadcasts Threatening Koran Texts by Mistake," *Ananova*.

[359] Olsen, "How Peaceful is Islam," *Christianity Today*, 21 September 2001.

he said, "Muslim terrorists have … a cosmic sense of justice or righteousness that permits anything in the name of God." Galli concluded his article with the following; "In this war against religious terrorism, Christians in particular should be able to act with both vigor and humility. As a religious people, we understand the frustration and anger that motivate the attacks, and we are particularly scandalized, again as a religious people, by terrorism employed in the name of God."

He asserted that evangelical backing of a secular nation in a war against terrorism does not violate the tenets of Christianity. "On this side of the kingdom, justice is impossible without some violence," he wrote.[360]

In a quest for a thoughtful response to the terrorist attacks, CT editors turned to Miroslav Volf, a professor of theology at Yale Divinity School. Volf delivered a speech to the United Nations annual prayer breakfast on the morning of September 11, only a few blocks away from the attacks. CT posted the text of the speech on September 21. In the address, Volf said religious people should recognize that the primary approach to conflict should be that of reconciliation, "the will to embrace the other, even the evil other, is a fundamental Christian obligation." Volf argued even though fear and anger encompasses religion-based conflict, "justice" alone should not be the goal. Rather, he said Christians should seek a positive, ongoing relationship with the Other. He said, "You will have justice only if you strive for something greater than justice, only if you strive after love."[361]

Tony Carnes also interviewed Volf on the issue of reconciliation, offering in the introduction: "Reconciliation is the last thing on the minds of most Americans – including Christians. We are angry." Volf replied that he also "felt we needed to go after them, that they needed

[360] Mark Galli, "Now What? A Christian Response to Terrorism," *Christianity Today*, 21 September 2001.
[361] Miroslav Volf, "After the Grave in the Air," *Christianity Today*, 21 September 2001.

to pay." Volf went on to say that Americans, including Christians, must "protect ourselves from the possibility of such an event from ever happening again." The Croatian professor said Christians such as Dietrich Bonhoeffer, who was involved in a plot to assassinate Hitler, "had the right perspective on such acts," insofar that "doing the right thing entailed doing the wrong thing." Volf explains:

> Taking a life is always the wrong thing. The choice Bonhoeffer had was doing the lesser of the evils. However the fact that one has to do evil and chooses the lesser one doesn't mean it becomes *not* evil. He must still repent of his sin. The self-righteousness with which we go after those who have assaulted us and the absence of any sense that we ourselves are implicated in their act to me is deeply troubling.[362]

Christianity Today After Sept. 11, 2001

Conflict:

In the months following the Sept 11 attacks, conflict articles dominated the coverage of Muslim-Christians encounters. The theme of Christian persecution continued as it had in previous years, but many of the articles pointed out heightened tensions arising from the attacks in the United States as well as the war on terror in Afghanistan.

For example, an October news brief told of riots in Nigeria in which at least 500 Muslims and Christians died. The article said fighting between the two religious groups was reportedly linked to Muslim Nigerians celebrating the attacks in New York and Washington, DC. The report said that one riot in Kano was sparked by a demonstration by 5,000 Muslim youth, and another in the city of Jos, in which 165 people were killed. The same news brief also mentioned the legal proceedings in Afghanistan involving accusation by the Taliban that eight foreign aid workers, including Americans Dayna Curry and

---

[362] Tony Carnes, "To Embrace the Enemy," *Christianity Today*, 21 September 2001.

Heather Mercer. They were accused by the regime of violating laws against the preaching of Christianity. Two additional articles appeared in the pages of *Christianity Today* about Mercer and Curry's plight after they were captured and held by the Taliban.

A month later, a short news item was published about the fear Christians in Pakistan felt over the possible backlash, including "ferocious assaults" in reaction to the U.S. war on terrorism in Afghanistan. The article cited one case in September where members of five Christian families were dragged into the streets of Rawalpindi and beaten by a mob. The article reports some churches hiring armed guards, and missionary organizations such as the Evangelical Alliance Mission evacuating their foreign staff.[363]

In the same issue, CT published an article about complaints from groups lobbying Congress for punitive action against the Sudanese government over the persecution of Christians in Sudan. The Sudan Coalition, made up of the National Association of Evangelicals, the Family Research Council, AFL-CIO, and others were urging further sanctions against Sudan when the attacks of Sept. 11 and its aftermath derailed its lobbying effort. The Sudanese government reportedly offered cooperation with the Bush administration in the war on terror in exchange for a cease-fire in the American push for capital market sanctions. As House Speaker Dennis Hastert scuttled the Sudan Peace Act in Congress, evangelical activists such as Gary Bauer complained that the trade-off between the U.S. and Sudan was tragic and "likely to increase suffering rather than ease it."[364]

Understanding:

One article published in the December 3 issue of CT fell into the category of "understanding." The article revolves around efforts in

---

[363] Stan Guthrie, "Christians Fear Muslim Backlash," *Christianity Today*, 12 November 2001, 30.

[364] Art Moore, "Justice Delayed," *Christianity Today*, 12 November 2001, 23.

Egypt to invigorate the country's Coptic Church. The church is suffering from a dwindling number of monks, and tensions over whether church resources should be used to shore up the existing Coptic community, or for outreach to the masses for its desert monasteries. The conflict is personified in the disagreements between Pope Shenouda and Father Matta el-Meskeen, whose decades-long disagreements have strained the unity of the Coptic Church.

Dialogue:

Philip Yancey where reprinted a letter from a Muslim "seeker," which constitutes the category of dialogue after the Sept. 11 attacks in the year 2001. The letter from a "moderately religious" Pakistani Muslim, faxed to Yancey on Sept. 12, tells of an individual who found it easier to study Islam with a critical eye while living in the United States. (It is unclear whether the letter is from a man or a woman.) The author speaks of investigating the claims of Christianity compared to that of Islam, and the disillusionment the person is feeling toward strands of militancy in the religion. "The terrible tragedy that happened yesterday in this country seems to be the logical outcome of teachings that tell you it's okay to reply in kind," the author wrote.[365]

But the letter-writer still feels some trepidation about developing relationships with American or Pakistani Christians. The letter closes by asking Yancey if "I would find loving and open-minded friends in the church? Would it be fair to say some people would put their guards up and won't want anything to do with someone who belongs to a different Asian Indian race? Someone who has a different color of skin and speaks with an accent?"[366]

---

[365] Philip Yancey, "Letter From a Muslim Seeker," *Christianity Today*, 3 December 2001, 80.
[366] Ibid.

Yancey tells the reader that the letter personalized "a conflict normally discussed in global terms." He said, "everything going on in the world took a different slant because of this letter." Instead of explicitly outlining what the evangelical community needs to do, Yancey lets the letter speak for itself in challenging the Christian reader to have an open, welcoming relationship with Muslims who are asking similar questions after Sept. 11.

Sojourners & World Magazines in 2001:

Sojourners ran eleven articles dealing with Muslim-Christian encounters during 2001. In the months prior to the Sept. 11 attacks, some of the most significant were dealt with the Middle East, American Muslim women, and the Christian nonviolence movement.

The article on the Middle East dealt with the power of memory among Israelis and Palestinians who have seen decades of violence. James Aageson of Concordia College, Minnesota argued that memory of wrongs and violence can lead to either peace or continued violence, and the direction those memories take is "fueled" by "religious narratives and theological claims that govern people's lives." Aageson was deeply critical of the idea that Israel has been given a right, in perpetuity, to the land it now occupies, to the detriment of Palestinians. He said that Christians, as well as Jews and Arabs, must reexamine how their memories are leading them toward a "spiral of violence" instead of peace and reconciliation.[367]

Another article on the Middle East by *Sojourners* editor-in-chief Jim Wallis, hoped to put a positive spin on efforts to bring about an end to decades of violence: "The good news in the Middle East today is that voices are emerging to call for nonviolence." Christian Peacemaker Teams (CPT) are praised in the article for "both a heroic and practical object of nonviolence in the Middle East," through their efforts to

---

[367] James W. Aageson, "Remember This," *Sojourners Magazine*, March-April 2001, 40.

stand alongside Palestinians in areas known for often bloody clashes such as Hebron. The article also said that similar efforts among Jewish and Muslim groups point to a trend of more calls for a nonviolent end to the conflict.[368] CPT was also the subject of a short news item in the same issue regarding their work in Hebron.[369]

Two items, a long article and a sidebar, examined the issue of Muslim women in the U.S. (including the choice of some to cover their heads with a *hijab*). The author argued that "discrimination is a common experience for many Muslims women," citing resistance by owners of a building in Claremont, California where a Muslim woman educator wanted to build a school. The article said the role of Muslim women is as diverse as the communities they come from. "A new role is evolving in terms of equality, which is good," said one interviewee, "On the other hand, we don't appreciate the Western model of sexual promiscuity, drinking, divorce. This is not equality in my book – its sexploitation."[370]

Following the Sept. 11 attacks, Sojourners printed a "religious response to terrorism" endorsed by more than 2,500 signers, ranging from evangelical and mainline ministers to Muslims and Buddhists. The document calls for the United States not to retaliate "out of anger and vengeance ... in ways that bring on even more loss of innocent life." It said America needs to avoid creating more violence and oppression by submitting to a world created in the terrorists' image. It calls for those living in the U.S. to "rededicate ourselves to global peace ... and the eradication of injustice that breeds rage and vengeance."[371]

---

[368] Jim Wallis, "Against Impossible Odds," *Sojourners Magazine*, September-October 2001, 20-28.

[369] Susannah Hunter, "On the Front Lines With Christian Peacemaker Teams," *Sojourners Magazine*, September-October 2001, 22.

[370] Pat McDonnell Twair, "Who is the Veiled Woman," *Sojourners Magazine*, May-June 2001, 40.

[371] "Deny Them Their Victory," *Sojourners Magazine*, November-December 2001, 26.

Another noteworthy *Sojourners* article by its editor-in-chief, Jim Wallis calls for the U.S. government not to bomb Afghanistan and risk hurting innocent civilians, but rather to feed the hungry in that country to remedy injustice and reduce the motivation for terrorist activity.[372]

In *World Magazine,* the immediate response was somewhat mixed. Before the Sept. 11 attacks, there were hardly any articles appearing in the periodical's pages that dealt with Muslims and Islam. One exception was the destruction of the Bamiyan Buddhas in Afghanistan, which Cal Thomas used as a case in point to illustrate the international outcry from over the loss of nation's cultural treasures, just as the outrage over the human rights abuses of the Taliban began to wane.[373] Following the attacks, *World* archives show a flood of news, information and commentary on Muslims and Islam.

Though *World's* coverage was in some ways extensive, there were a few missteps noted by other publications. A *Christianity Today* item posted on CT's website tells of a *World* editorial published on September 22, 2001 that was excoriated by the *Weekly Standard* as "over the edge" and "contemptible."[374] The magazine's publisher, Joel Belz, apologized for the placement of the word "The Wages of Sin" below a picture of the burning World Trade Center towers. "I can understand how some readers thought we were also saying that the victims had gotten exactly what they deserved," Belz wrote, "the blame belongs to the terrorists – and only the terrorists."[375]

In the same September 22 issue, *World* editor Marvin Olasky wrote that the root cause of the terrorist attack was original sin. "Not their [the victims] personal sin, we must hasten to say," he asserted. "We are not dealing with cowards. It takes a kind of bravery to take over

---

[372] Wallis, "A Light in the Darkness," *Sojourners Magazine,* November-December 2001, 7-9.

[373] Cal Thomas, "Idols for Destruction," *World Magazine,* 17 March 2001.

[374] Ted Olsen, "Weblog: *World* Publisher Apologizes for 'Clumsy' Editorial," *Christianity Today,* 5 October 2001.

[375] Ibid.

airplanes and commit suicide with them," wrote Olasky, "It will take bravery on our part to keep the 911 murderers from murdering again."[376]

The next month, *World* published an issue replete with reference material on Islam and the history of terrorism. The October 27 issue included timelines on the development of Islam - beginning c.1900 B.C. with Abraham, and ending in 2001 when "About 6,000 die in [a] Wahhabi Muslim attack on the United States." The issue also contained book recommendations, and a fairly comprehensive list of terrorist attacks in Western countries by Muslim and non-Muslim groups since 1968. Also listed were 31 Muslim leaders "worth knowing about," ranging from Burhanuddin Rabbani to Nihad Awad to Sayyid M. Syeed.[377]

In the same issue, Olasky argued that Christians must assess "whether most Muslims will be willing and able to join a new coalition [against terror], or whether Islam is a breeding ground for terrorists."[378] Also appearing in the October 27 issue was a polemical article comparing Islam negatively to Christianity. Olasky credited the theological tension between the Trinity's "one and the many" with pushing "Christians to bold a society that emphasizes both unity and diversity." On the other hand, he wrote the Islamic "emphasis on *tawhid*" is connected to the rise in dictatorships in Muslim countries. On social and legal issues, Olasky argued that Islam does not "understand compassion – suffering with the poor – in the way Christianity does," and offers cruel punishments, such as amputation for thieves. Olasky also attempts to draw a direct connection between the religion of Islam and terrorism. He said some Muslims, such as the Sept. 11 hijackers who are said to have partied the night before the

---

[376] Marvin Olasky, "9/11: If We Call, God Will Answer," *World magazine*, 22 September 2001.

[377] Tim Graham, "Appetite for Evil," *World Magazine*, 27 October 2001. Marvin Olasky, "Important Dates in the Development of Islam," *World Magazine*, 27 October 2001.

[378] Olasky, "A Cold War for the 21st Century," *World Magazine*, 27 October 2001.

attacks, look for a "get-out-of-jail-free card" through "one fiery ending purportedly making up for a multitude of sins."[379]

2002: Aftershock and Response

Total Articles: 47

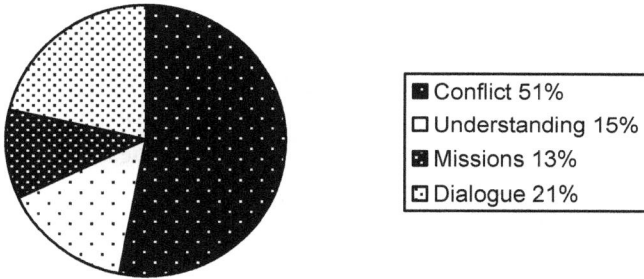

Conflict: 25   Understanding: 7   Missions: 5   Dialogue: 10

Trends in *Christianity Today*'s coverage during 2002

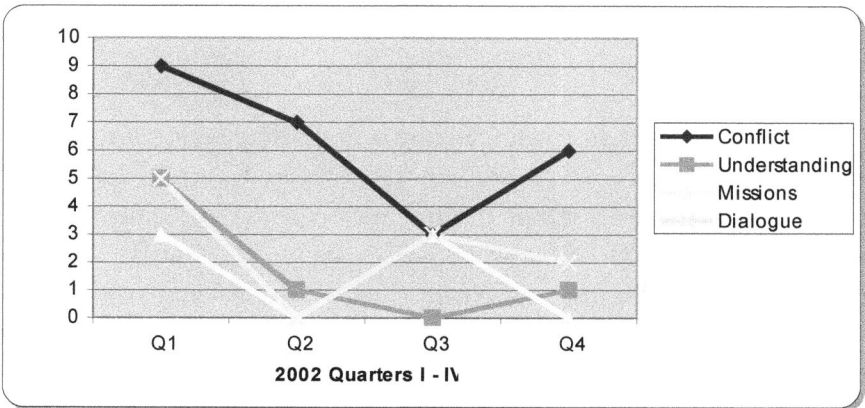

---

379 _____. "Brutality and Dictatorship: How Islam Affects Society," *World Magazine*, 27 October 2001.

The above chart shows the number of articles in each category as they appear in CT from the first quarter through the last of 2002. "Q1" represents the first portion of 2002, displaying a sharp spike in the number of Muslim-related articles in CT across all categories, with an especially steep rise in the number of conflict-related articles. The chart also shows that although coverage in the subject area dropped somewhat for those issues between April, May and June of 2002, "conflict" remained high.

The first anniversary of the Sept. 11 attacks fell into the third quarter of 2002 ("Q3" on the chart), and the graph shows the editors of CT publishing an equal number of articles dealing with conflict, dialogue and missions/evangelism in that quarter. In the last quarter of 2002, these trends once again diverge, with a rise in the number of conflict articles, and a reduction in dialogue. The total word count for 2002 was more than 46,000 (compared to less than 18,000 words in 2001). The dramatic rise in the number of articles and the word count shows the CT editors' deep interest in covering Islam and Muslims during the year after the attacks.

First Quarter 2002:

One of the first items in CT during 2002 that dealt with Muslim-Christian encounters was a column by respected evangelical activist Chuck Colson. In an attempt to give readers a way of thinking about Islam's relationship to Christianity, Colson paints a dichotomy between the two religions and their adherents as an ideological and civilizational clash. In his discussion of the fundamental differences between the beliefs that motivate Muslims and those of Christians, Colson wrote: "fundamentalist Muslim leaders are utopian; they seek the perfect society by strictly enforcing Islamic law. But this utopian worldview has already brought tyranny and disaster, just as communist utopianism led to the tragic deaths of tens of millions in the former Soviet Union."[380]

This view of Islamic fundamentalism as replacing the evil of communism is a reflection of the viewpoint asserted in articles printed in CT during previous years. However, Colson asks and answers an emerging theological question within evangelical discourse: whether the deity of Christianity is held in common with Islam. "We need a bracing dose of realism: like it or not, ancient worldviews are again struggling for domination; we do not all worship the same God."[381]

This question was expanded into a cover story for the February issue of CT, in an article titled "Is the God of Muhammad the Father of Jesus?" by Timothy George. This article, which runs more than 4,000 words, examines the theological understanding in each religion as to the nature of God: his work in history, his relationship to creation, the avenues of revelation, and so on. George resolves the question in a more nuanced way than Colson by asserting the answer is both yes and no: "Christians and Muslims can together affirm many important truths about this great God – his oneness, eternity, power, majesty. As the Qur'an puts it, he is "the Living, the Everlasting, the All-High, the All Glorious' (2:256)." However, George asserted that the line is drawn at the divinity of Christ and the personhood of the Holy Spirit, which are critical to the Christian understanding of God's nature: "Apart from the Incarnation and the Trinity, it is possible to know *that* God is, but not *who* God is."[382]

In crafting a response to Islam in the wake of the September 11 attacks, it is not surprising that evangelicals turned first to the doctrinal issues at hand, just as they had during the 1940's and 1950's to define both what they stand for and what they oppose. However, setting up a

---

[380] Chuck Colson, "Drawing the Battle Lines," 7 January 2002, *Christianity Today*, 80.

[381] Ibid.

[382] Timothy George, "Is the God of Muhammad the Father of Jesus?" *Christianity Today*, 4 February 2002, 28.

theological fence between Islam and Christianity was but one response to the challenge of the Other as experienced by evangelicals.

In an effort to complement George's article, Wheaton College professor James Lewis wrote in CT's February 2002 issue: "when discussing whether Christians and Muslims worship the same God, we must remember that God does not deal with theologies; he deals with persons." Lewis goes on to say that God hears the prayers of those who understand him in only limited ways, and that includes Muslims. He also takes the reaction to the Other a step further by advocating closer bonds between Christians and Muslims: "In this new and dangerous epoch of world history, which threatens to embroil us in religious wars and civilizational clashes we may do well to seek Muslim prayer partners and together beseech the true, one and only God to have mercy on us."[383]

Another question haunting evangelical discourse before and after Sept. 11 was whether Islam is a religion of peace. An article by Tyndale Seminary theologian James Beverley tackled the looming question about the nature of Islam by asserting that there is a struggle within the religion itself to define whether it advocates human rights, peace and tolerance, or heads down a path of violence and tyranny. Beverly said the answer is much more complex than a simple yes or no: "Muslims are in the midst of a struggle for the soul of Islam. We would be wise as Christians humbled by out own past, to remember that as we seek to understand and engage Muslims today out of love for Christ."[384]

---

[383] James Lewis, "Does God Hear Muslims' Prayers?" 4 February 2002, 30.

[384] James A. Beverley, "Is Islam a Religion of Peace?" *Christianity Today*, 7 January 2002, 32.

Second Quarter 2002

CT took a break for the most part from the in-depth coverage of Islam and Muslims during the second quarter of 2002. During this time, seven conflict articles appeared, mostly dealing with ongoing Muslim-Christian around the world. The largest conflict article dealt with the struggle for freedom by a Filipino pastor condemned to death by the Saudi government for blasphemy.[385]

During this quarter, there was also one article appearing in the category of "understanding" and none in the categories of "missions" and "dialogue." In the "understanding" article, popular evangelical author Phillip Yancey suggests that the moral decay of the West is part of why many in the Muslim world hate the United States. He said Christians can temper how much of this hatred bleeds over onto evangelicals by resisting the decadence and moral decay that is seen in Western media, and promoting programs and outreaches designed to "care for the downtrodden and [display] love for enemies."[386]

Another dialogue article examines the direct response evangelicals should have in response to Islam and Muslims. During an interview, Fuller Seminary President Richard Mouw argued that Christians should recognize and affirm certain truths that may exist within Islam as a product of "common grace," something given by God to everyone regardless of religion. Mouw is careful not to violate the evangelical tenet of Christian exclusivity, but rather encourages tolerance and a broader perspective of the issue: "There are truths in other religions. But that's a different question from whether all religions are equally valid ways to God."[387] Mouw said, "We have a tendency to dehumanize and supernaturalize the enemy so that we're dealing with absolute radical evil. The tendency then is, if we can see our enemies as satanic, then we no longer have to acknowledge their

[385] Jeff Sellers, "How to Confront a Theocracy," *Christianity Today*, 8 July 2002, 34.

[386] Philip Yancey, "Why Do They Hate Us?" *Christianity Today*, 1 April 2002, 80.

[387] Richard Mouw, "The Uncommon Benefit of Common Grace," *Christianity Today*, 8 July 2002, 50.

humanness." He adds, "I certainly don't have qualms about the use of military violence in response to terrorism. But in all of that we need to honor and acknowledge the humanity of the people we are fighting."[388]

Third Quarter 2002:

During this quarter, the drop in the number of conflict articles was met by the rise in the number of missions and dialogue articles, with a total of three articles each for those categories. (There were no articles in the category of understanding during this quarter.)

The longest and most significant article dealing with missions and evangelism claimed that in the year since the attacks, there has been "a fresh momentum" among evangelistic efforts in the Muslim world, and a general rise in the number of converts from Islam to Christianity. Missionaries quoted in the article say an accurate count of Muslim converts is often hard to assess because of the persecution they could face. Even so, the significant rise in the numbers of Christians in Muslim countries is reported as occurring from the Berber minority of Algeria to the burgeoning Christian minority in Indonesia.[389]

One article deals with the concern for 15,000 "secret believers" living in Kashmir, Pakistan. A Roman Catholic leader is quoted as saying: "There are more Christians in Kashmir than on the record... They have faith in Jesus but don't come out. They are not bold about it. Their number goes into [the] thousands in the rural areas. We don't want to advertise. It has serious repercussions."[390]

In contrast to the somewhat ecumenical and theological discussions of the early part of the 2002, a "conflict" article appeared in the September issue on the effort by a Fuller Seminary graduate to

---

[388] Ibid.

[389] Stan Guthrie, "Doors Into Islam," *Christianity Today*, 9 September 2002, 34.

[390] Manpreet Singh, "Harassed Kashmir Christians Reach Out to Discreet Muslims," *Christianity Today*, 9 September 2002, 26.

attack the credibility of the Quran. The article reports that Jay Smith was actively debating Muslims as to the integrity of the Quran, which he said has "huge errors" in it. Smith maintains, "My goal is to eradicate the whole edifice of Islam so that the [Muslims] can then look for the alternative."[391]

Two dialogue articles stand out in this quarter's coverage of Muslim-Christian encounters. The first deals with the competition between the World Council of Churches and the World Evangelical Fellowship over "ecumenical" relationships with the Muslim world. The WCC is criticized by the author, a Drew University theology professor, for "carrying on its ideological programs, syncretism, universalism, and the greenest of the green world's ecological agendas." The author suggests the WCC's backing of "government-to-government" debt relief to Zimbabwe would primarily benefit the country's president Robert Mugabe and "his cronies." He compares this to the WEF's efforts backing successful, grassroots micro-enterprise programs in Indonesia and eliciting support for religious liberties from Prime Minister Mahathir bin Mohamed in Malaysia. The author argued that liberal church institutions such as the WCC are in a state of decline and organizations such as the WEF should maintain course in representing an alternative stream of Christianity to the international community, particularly in the Muslim world.[392]

Fourth Quarter 2002:

The final quarter of 2002 saw a small increase in the number of conflict articles and a drop in the number of mission, understanding and dialogue articles. However, the nature of the conflict articles dealt primarily with worldwide Muslim-Christian violence, including the

[391] Stan Guthrie, "Deconstructing Islam," *Christianity Today*, 9 September 2002, 37.
[392] Thomas Oden, "Whither Christian Unity? *Christianity Today*, 5 August 2002, 46.

upheaval that left thousands dead and tens of thousands homeless in Nigeria's Plateau state and its capital Jos.[393]

One article dealt with the pressures faced by Iraq's Christian community under Saddam Hussein's regime. It reports many Christian groups in the country have sought support from Saddam's regime out of fear of militant Islamists. The author said Islamic extremists were believed to be responsible for the beheading of a 71-year-old nun at the Sacred Heart of Jesus monastery in Baghdad. One elder in the Assyrian Presbyterian community said, "Anti-Christianity has expanded a lot … They make it public: 'We don't like you.' You hear it when they are preaching on Fridays."[394]

There was one article that specifically called for mobilization (rounding out the "mobilization" articles' appearance of once per quarter during 2002). This particular item told of pressures from the Egyptian government and persecution from Egyptian Muslims faced by the Coptic and Protestant community. The article encourages evangelicals to write Secretary of State Colin Powell and the Egyptian ambassador in Washington to offer relief to Christians in Egypt.[395]

Also under the dialogue category was an Ecumenical News International article about Nigerian Muslims and Christians meeting together in the nation's capital of Abuja to discuss conflict resolution and reduce interreligious violence. The article said that even though both religious groups desire an end to the rising bloodshed and instability, "they were sharply divided over Shari'ah. Christians told their Muslim counterparts that Islamic laws should not apply to Christians. Muslim leaders in turn accused Christians of intolerance. Yet both sides said they would pursue peaceful coexistence.[396]

[393] Stan Guthrie, "A Blast of Hell," *Christianity Today*, 7 October 2002, 16.
[394] Guthrie, "Keeping Their heads Down," *Christianity Today*, 18 November 2002.
[395] Jeff M. Sellers, "Heightened Hostilities," 9 December 2002, 58.
[396] "Violence-Weary Muslims and Christians Talk Peace in Nigeria," *Christianity Today*, 18 November 2002, 34.

The final dialogue article of the year was an editorial by the CT staff calling for evangelicals to be careful about the words they use when speaking about Muslims. The article cited an ABC News/Beliefnet poll that found white evangelicals were "more likely than other Americans to think that Islam encourages violence." The editorial laid a certain amount of responsibility at the feet of evangelical leaders such as Pat Robertson, Jerry Falwell, Jerry Vines and Franklin Graham for comments that hurt the evangelical stance toward Islam and Muslims.[397]

The editorial said that before the Sept. 11 attacks, Muslims were seen by some in the evangelical community as "one of our few international allies in fighting the materialism and decadence that tear at the fabric of families." The editorial advocates building goodwill among Muslims: "if we hope to demonstrate the love and saving power of Christ to Muslims, we're going to have to cease the name-calling and reach out in love – yes, especially to those who in some respects are now considered our 'enemies.'"[398]

Sojourners & World Magazines:

During 2002, the semi-monthly *Sojourners* published 19 items related to Islam or Muslim – Christian encounters, including a variety of book reviews and short news articles. Among the event-related pieces was an article on the murder of Balbir Singh Sodhi, cited as the first "backlash" killing related to the Sept. 11 attacks.[399] Another tells about efforts to build interfaith dialogue between Muslims and Christians on the violence-ridden island of Mindanao in the

---

[397] "Verbal Attacks on Islam Sabotage Evangelism," *Christianity Today*, 9 December 2002, 28.

[398] Ibid.

[399] Rose Marie Berger, "United We Stand," *Sojourners Magazine*, January-February 2002, 34.

Philippines.[400] Still another called for more Christian and U.S. diplomatic attention on the persecution of Christians in places such as India and Pakistan.[401]

But the most significant contribution of *Sojourners* was a series of commentaries by editor-in-chief, Jim Wallis. In the first issue of 2002, Wallis outlines the dilemma faced by "Christian peacemakers" who have a commitment to nonviolent conflict resolution. In the issue's cover story, Wallis wrote that Christian peacemakers must "be realistic" in understanding that terrorists are planning further violence on a massive scale, and stopping them "involves using some kind of force." Wallis said he reviewed such Christian and non-Christian peacemaking sources, including Dietrich Bonhoeffer, Jacques Ellul, and Gandhi in search of an ethic for a balance between pacifism and a hawkish approach to terrorism.

Wallis concluded that Christians should "explore a theology for global police forces," which he presumes would offer a more constrained response to terrorism than a military solution. For example, Wallis worries about civilian casualties in the war against the Taliban in Afghanistan. He suggests an internationally-run police force with a global authority is a better alternative than military action, arguing that such a force could "de-fang" and defeat terror networks such as al-Qaida "without bombing an entire country."[402]

In the March-April edition of the magazine, Wallis elaborates on his views of religion, violence and peacemaking by asserting that the problem is not with "fundamentalism" itself among world religions, rather it is the tendency of some to seek a theocracy. In addition to linking Osama bin Laden and al-Qaida with a dangerous theocratic

---

[400] Mary Ann Cejka, "A Miracle in Mindanao, *Sojourners Magazine*, July-August 2002, 42-44.

[401] Ivy George, "The Persecuted Body," *Sojourners Magazine*, March-April 2002, 42-45.

[402] Jim Wallis, "Hard Questions for Peacemakers," *Sojourners Magazine*, January February 2002, 29-33.

worldview, Wallis includes some prominent evangelicals under this umbrella: "In my view, al-Qaeda, the Taliban, and American fundamentalists like Jerry Falwell and Pat Robertson are indeed theocrats asking that their religious agenda be enforced by the power of the state," adding that this stream of fundamentalism "too easily justifies violence as a toll for implementing its agenda." Wallis argued that "genuine faith" does not include "taking over the mechanisms of the state."[403]

Toward the end of the year, Wallis reasserted his nonviolence by voicing opposition to the impending war in Iraq. Wallis argued that "neither international law or 'just war' doctrine allow pre-emptive military action by one state against another," even if it is acknowledged that Saddam Hussein was an evil ruler. Wallis warned that war in Iraq would fuel hatred in the Arab world, "leading to new volunteers for further terrorist attacks against the United States.[404]

Though many pages in *Sojourners* dealt with Christian peacemaking and the challenge of Islamic terrorism, the magazine did not publish articles that wrestled with the theological challenge of Islam itself, or the relationship of Christians to Muslims on a religious level.

World Magazine, a weekly, published 100 articles with content on Islam and Muslims - about the same rate as the *Sojourners.* However, the editors of the periodical went in an entirely different direction in their reporting and commentary in this area.

It was noted earlier that *World* apologized for inflammatory remarks in the weeks after Sept. 11, 2001.[405] During 2002, just as *Christianity Today* called for friendly outreach to Muslims and *Sojourners* emphasized peacemaking, *World* stressed polemics over dialogue. *World*

403 ————. "Fundamentalism and the Modern World," *Sojourners Magazine,* March-April 2002, 20-26.
404 Wallis, "Disarm Iraq ... Without War," *Sojourners Magazine,* November-December 2002, 7-8.
405 Olsen, "Weblog: World Publisher Apologizes for 'Clumsy Editorial."

remained resolutely unapologetic in the reporting of comments by Pat Robertson Jerry Falwell and Franklin Graham that Muslims considered hurtful. Commenting on a *60 Minutes* story in which Jerry Falwell referred to Muhammad as a "terrorist," *World* editor Marvin Olasky defended the high-profile minister: "Jerry Falwell spoke bluntly, but he is a plain-spoken Baptist preacher, not a diplomat." Olasky reserved criticism for the television show's producers, which he accused of "shoddy, bigoted journalism" because they included the sound bite in a segment on evangelicals and Israel. [406]

Olasky offered a similar defense of remarks by Jerry Vines, a Baptist pastor from Jacksonville, Florida. In June 2002, Vines remarked, "Islam was founded by Muhammad, a demon-possessed pedophile who had 12 wives – and his last one was a 9-year-old girl." The New York Times, the Washington Post and other publications roundly condemned the comments as hate speech. However, Olasky said there was "no reason for journalists to be shocked, shocked that Mr. Vines, a former SBC president, took a strong stand against Islam." The editorial went on to say, "Mr. Vines was not diplomatic, but we have plenty of diplomats whispering sweet nothings about Islam." Olasky defended Vines, mentioning the SBC leader "tempered his tone" after returning to his church. "I love Muslim people, I have found many of them to be kind, gentle and loving people," said Vines. [407]

Throughout 2002, Olasky and the editors of *World* continued to dismiss efforts by Christians to improve interfaith relations with Muslims. In a review of books on Islam by evangelicals such as Ravi Zacharias, Bruce McDowell and Chawkat Moucarry, Olasky wrote: "All three books make it clear that those who say Muslims and

---

[406] Olasky, "Lights, Camera, Exploitation," *World Magazine*, 19 October 2002.

[407] _____. "Bias is Back: The Post-9/11 Talibanization of U.S. Religious Conservatives Continues," *World Magazine*, 17 August 2002.

Westerners can all get along if we're just nice to each other are thinking like children."[408]

World's combative stance was also directed at what the editors perceived as a threat from secularists. They feared theologically conservative Christians would be equated with Islamic terrorists (similar to what had appeared *Sojourners*).[409] Mainstream journalists, particularly at the New York Times, are seen as the worst offenders in an article on "anti-Christian bigotry:" The April 27, 2002 cover story cited Times columnists Anthony Lewis equating John Ashcroft and Osama bin Laden, Bill Keller referring to the "Taliban wing of the American right," and Maureen Dowd "equating biblical requirements concerning male leadership with the 'Taliban obliteration of women."[410] The same article also cited a February 2002 Atlantic Monthly story, which is characterized in *World* as saying "concern about Islam is overblown, for 'the big problem cult' of the 21st century will be Christianity."

In a year-in-review article, after citing examples of cultural struggles between liberal secularists and conservative Christians, author Gene Edward Veith concludes:

> 2002 was a year of cultural transition. But as postmodernism falls apart, it is not yet clear what will take its place. It may be that Christianity will get branded as a terrorist religion, like that of the radical Muslims, in which case things will go from bad to worse, as secularism is either intensified or is sanctified into a new Interfaith religion. Or the culture may recover at least

---

[408] _____. "Spring Treadmill: Books to Get Our Minds in Shape," *World Magazine*, 23 March 2002.

[409] Wallis, "Fundamentalism and the Modern World."

[410] Olasky, "Anti-Christian Bigotry," *World Magazine*, 27 April 2002.

some of its heritage. At any rate, we are approaching a cultural moment that may be ripe for Christian influence.[411]

2003: Cultivating New Discourse

Total articles: 21

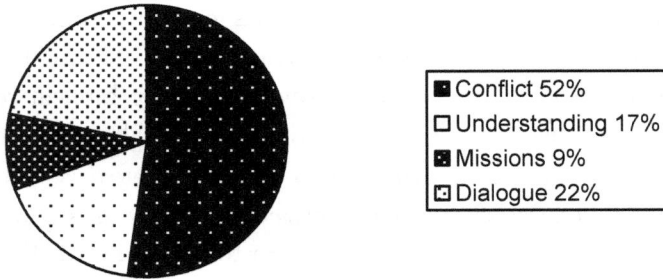

Conflict: 12   Understanding: 4 Missions: 2   Dialogue: 5

Conflict:

Noteworthy articles in the conflict category include a December editorial on the use of the word "persecution" to describe pressures faced by evangelicals in the United States. The editorial offers a reality check to American Christians who complain of injustices in the corporate world and in government policies. The editors maintain that those pressures are minor compared to the true persecution faced by Christians in the Muslim world. "How can we tell a fellow Christian hanging from a cross in Sudan that the American Civil Liberties Union is 'persecuting' us?" said the editorial, "How would the story of our church's zoning woes sound to a Christian sister in Pakistan who has

---

[411] Gene Edward Veith, "Culture Year-in-Review," *World Magazine*, 28 December 2002.

been raped and forcibly married to a Muslim neighbor?" The authors of the piece say American evangelicals can use terms such as "injustice, liberalism run amok, or discrimination" to describe the wrongs they face in the U.S. However, they say calling it persecution when others around the world face torture and death, "demeans their sacrifice."[412]

Another conflict article appeared during the same month to examine the book *A Season in Bethlehem: Unholy War in a Sacred Place* by Newsweek reporter Joshua Hammer. The book deals with the radicalization of Muslim groups in the West Bank town, and the problems created by the Israeli occupation and Muslim militants create among the remaining Palestinian Christians. One portion of the article tells of how the Tanzim militia invaded Arab Christian homes to gain firing positions, as well as to "radicalize" local Christians by pulling them into the conflict.[413] A companion interview piece discussed the erosion of the Palestinian Christian presence in the region as observed by Hammer.[414]

In June and September 2003, CT dealt with the future of Iraqi Christians in a post-Saddam Iraq. The June editorial discussed the need for religious freedom in the new government to protect the minority that had previously been sheltered by Saddam's government.[415] The lengthier article in September spelled out what life was like for Christians who "enjoyed relative freedom" under Saddam's regime, noting, "many Christians were members of the [ruling] Baath party." However, the Christian community wonders what may lie ahead under a government that is perhaps dominated by the previously persecuted Shi'a majority. The article also notes evangelical relief efforts may not go over well if they are seen as a part of the American occupation, rather than an effort by Iraqi Christians. In spite of all these concerns,

---

[412] "Persecution is a Holy Word," *Christianity Today*, December 2003, 32.

[413] David Neff, "Thugs in Jesus' Hometown," December 2003, 34.

[414] Neff, "Editor's Bookshelf: The Erosion Continues," December 2003, 61.

[415] "The Mother of All Liberties," *Christianity Today*, June 2003, 30.

one minister offered some reassurances, "Don't worry about Christians in Iraq ... We've been here for 1,800 years."[416]

Another article called for evangelical political mobilization to put pressure on the Bush administration to recognize the persecution of Christians in Sudan. It outlined instances of violence in the Upper Nile region, and provided addresses for the State Department and White House, encouraging evangelicals to urge the administration to implement sanctions under the Sudan Peace Act.[417] The remainder of the conflict articles dealt primarily with interreligious violence and the persecution of Christians in, for example Nigeria, Pakistan, the Ivory Coast and Uzbekistan.

Understanding:

The dwindling ancient Christian communities of Turkey were the subject of the most substantial article in the "understanding" category. The article attempted to put the decline in Asia Minor's Christian population in context by describing the wars and demographic shifts that have occurred in the predominantly Muslim region over the past century. A Freedom House fellow traveling with the author described the Upper Mesopotamian region with its all-but-abandoned sites and churches as an "ancient Christian museum," as many of the Christian inhabitants have migrated to Europe and the United States.[418]

An April review of a documentary on St. Francis called *Reluctant Saint*, criticized the film for being too sentimental, avoiding issues that might not sit well with a modern, secular audience. In the case of Francis's trip to Egypt during the crusades, the reviewer said the film avoided the mendicant monk's agenda of proselytization when he

---

[416] Kevin Begos, "Other Baghdad battles Ahead for Christians," *Christianity Today*, September 2003, 29.

[417] Jeff M. Sellers, "Submitting to Islam – Or Dying," *Christianity Today*, October 2003, 100.

[418] Thomas C. Oden, "Death Watch," *Christianity Today*, 21 January 2003, 44.

crossed enemy lines to visit the warring sultan. The author maintained that, in reality, the sultan's religious advisors wanted to behead Francis for blasphemy, and Francis eventually left after realizing the Muslim leader wasn't interested in converting – facts not mentioned in the documentary.[419]

Missions/Evangelism:

Two articles appeared under the category of Muslim Missions and Evangelism in 2003. The first was an interview with Georg Taubman, a Shelter Now relief worker who was kidnapped by the Taliban in 2002, along with seven other Westerners (including Heather Mercer and Dayna Curry). Taubman returned to Afghanistan two years after his abduction, telling CT that he went back to help rebuild the country after the hard-line Taliban rulers were overthrown. He maintained that he, along with Mercer and Curry, never overtly proselytized during their previous tenure in the war-torn country, but did answer questions about their faith if asked.[420]

The other missions/evangelism article in this year dealt with the launch of relief efforts by evangelical groups in Iraq. Due to the precarious security situation faced by both relief workers and local Christians, representatives of a number of the relief organizations say they were forgoing mass evangelism techniques through the media and rallies in favor of a focus humanitarian assistance. One Southern Baptist mission board worker said they were funneling relief through local churches, and relying on Iraqi Christians for "verbal evangelism."[421]

---

[419] Mark Galli, "Reimagining Francis," *Christianity Today*, April 2003, 107.

[420] Stan Guthrie, "Return to Kabul," *Christianity Today*, 21 January 2003, 52.

[421] Dawn Herzog and Deann Alford, "No Strings Attached," *Christianity Today*, June 2003, 44.

Dialogue:

In July, CT reported on a "hastily called meeting" regarding disparaging comments toward Islam by some of the most well known evangelical leaders. In particular, the article notes that "media questioned" the appearance of Franklin Graham at a Good Friday event at the Pentagon. The meeting included representatives of the National Association of Evangelicals and the Institute for Religion and Democracy, and was centered on developing a set of guidelines for Muslim-Christian dialogue. The three-page document calling for leaders to "tone down" their language and speak to Muslim leaders drew mixed reaction from the evangelical community. Fuller Seminary's Dudley Woodberry is quoted as being "basically pleased" with the outline, while suggesting it needed "fine tuning."

Roy Oksnevad of Wheaton College's Ministries to Muslims was more pessimistic, saying they were of limited value and that "there is a dark side to Islam, and frankly, I've never met a Muslim who understood the concept of the Trinity." Graham had been invited to the May meeting with the NAE and IRD, but could not attend. The article reports that other leaders who have made controversial statements, including Jerry Falwell and Pat Robertson were not invited.[422]

An article appearing in April 2003 tackled conservative theology as it relates to the nation of Israel and what that means for evangelicals and the Middle East. The author, a professor at Jordan Evangelical Seminary in Amman, argued that there are both conditional and unconditional requirements set forth in the Abrahamic Covenant. He said Christian Zionists often emphasize the unconditional requirements, while Palestinian Christians often emphasize the conditional. The author said that "Palestinians as Arabs are not accursed sons of Ishmael destined to be eternal archenemies of Israel ... God promised to *bless* Ishmael." He said that "the Law" demands just treatment of non-Israelites living within the borders of Israel, and

---

[422] Stricherz, "Evangelicals Advise on Muslim Dialogue."

"Christians cannot succeed in fulfilling our biblical mandate to be peacemakers, however, unless we take more balanced theological and political positions on this issue."[423]

A dialogue article in May reported on the work of Christian Peacemaker Teams in Iraq before and during the coalition invasion of the country (the group had been criticized in previous issues of CT). The article quotes CPT leaders as denying they were acting as "human shields." However the actions of the group indicate otherwise: "CPT said volunteers visited orphanages, hospitals and water treatment facilities to protect them from coalition air strikes. Every day CPT sent the Pentagon and members of the Senate Foreign Relations Committee a fax about staff members' locations. It also obtained the Iraqi government's permission to enter some government-run facilities."[424]

Sojourners & World Magazines

Only eight articles fell into the category of Muslim-Christian encounters during 2003, less than half the number of articles the previous year. In the first issue of the year, *Sojourners* published an article by Charles Kimball that deeply criticized those in the evangelical community who delivered "inflammatory" remarks, including Falwell, Robertson and Franklin Graham. The lead sentence of the article condemned Falwell's characterization of Muhammad as a "terrorist" as "hateful, ignorant, arrogant, irresponsible, and destructive." Kimball argued that similar remarks feed Muslim extremism, put Christian relief workers at risk, and destroy efforts to "build bridges of understanding and cooperation."

Whereas *World* editors feared equivocation from secularists, Kimball offered that Falwell and bin Laden shared certain things in

---

[423] Mark Harlan, "A Middle Way in the Middle East," *Christianity Today*, April 2003, 84.

[424] Carol Lowes, "Mercy in Baghdad," *Christianity Today*, May 2003, 27.

common, "Like Osama bin Laden, Falwell believes that God was actively involved in causing the destruction of the World Trade Center and the Pentagon," albeit in different ways. Whereas *World* defended comments Muslims would find hurtful as merely undiplomatic, the *Sojourners* commentary called for a stop to the fiery rhetoric: "This kind of hateful, destructive language is deeply offensive to us as well, it does not represent the teachings of Jesus or the ministry to which we are called."[425]

Additionally, *Sojourners* printed a short news item titled "Not a Monolithic Bloc" about a letter sent by prominent evangelical leaders calling on the Bush administration to deal "even-handedly" between Israel and Palestinians in the Middle East peace process.[426] It also published a substantial article on the Bush administration's "road map" for the peace process, concluding that: "Extremists on both sides must realize that the land God promised to the descendants of Abraham belongs to them both, and that each dream of expelling the other must be given up."[427] (A May 11, 2002 *World* article offered the opposite tone: "whether or not today's Israelis necessarily have a God-specified right to the real estate they now possess, they certainly have a right to it in line with the Parable of Talents [Matthew 25] …they have turned a land of sand and poverty into a country of computer chips and honey. They have formed an island of democracy within a sea of dictatorship.")[428]

As *Christianity Today* and Sojourners reduced their coverage of Islam and Muslim-Christian encounters in 2003, *World Magazine* increased their coverage on the subject to more than 120 articles. Nearly half of those articles dealt in some way with the war in Iraq and

---

[425] Charles Kimball, "Osama and Me," *Sojourners Magazine*, January-February 2003, 17-18.

[426] "Not a Monolithic Bloc: Many U.S. Evangelicals Seek an 'Even-Handed' Middle East Policy," *Sojourners Magazine*, July-August 2003, 24.

[427] Duane Shank, "Road Map or Dead End?" *Sojourners Magazine*, July-August 2003, 15.

[428] Olasky, "Squandered Inheritance," *World Magazine*, 11 May 2002.

the rebellion against the occupation by Muslim insurgents. Noteworthy among articles on Iraq is a news item on then coalition administrator L. Paul Bremer approving "some form of Shariah law" without provision for "the chopping off of hands," in the new Iraqi constitution.[429]

Another article argued that Christians should "pray that [Iraqis] will not take their religion too seriously in the days ahead." The claimed many Muslims in Iraq are nominal and secularized; not adhering to the calls for religious violence called for by certain Sunni and Shiite leaders. The author wrote "the fewer fanatics we find in Iraq the better," regarding the safety of American troops.[430]

The remaining articles were roughly divided between items on Christian persecution abroad, and the cultural challenges in the United States. One example of international Muslim-Christian conflict reported in *World* was the fatal shooting in Yemen of three Southern Baptist missionary hospital workers by a man who reportedly told authorities "he shot the Americans because they were preaching Christianity in a Muslim country."[431]

The domestic articles illustrate the continual positioning of *World* editors and reporters in response to both Muslim-Americans and the forces of secularism (seen primarily in the guise of mainstream journalists). In one article, Gene Edward Veith argued that if the works-righteousness based system of Islam offers no ultimate assurance of salvation except through violent jihad, then it should be no surprise that the religion breeds militarism among its adherents. Veith supports this by saying Sept. 11 lead hijacker Mohammed Atta developed a "serious pornography addiction," but the "gospel of jihad" eased their fears of eternal damnation. The article also cited the spree

---

[429] "Except for 'The Chopping Off of Hands,' Bremer is Fine With Shariah," *World Magazine*, 22 November 2003.

[430] Joel Belz, "Pray For Nominalism," *World Magazine*, 10 May 2003.

[431] Edward E. Plowman, "Not a 'Senseless Waste," *World* Magazine, 11 January 2003.

of immoral behavior by the hijackers in the days leading up to the Sept. 11 attacks.[432]

Another apparent assault on Muslim theology came in the form of name-calling by a *World* headline writer. The short news item told of the approval by a leading Malaysian religious adviser of cellular text messaging on a mobile phone as a means of a Muslim man proclaiming a divorce to his wife. The headline referred to those involved as "high-tech Neanderthals."[433]

A number of *World* articles point to the emerging view among its editors of evangelicals as singled out by both Muslims, their defenders in the secular press, and even other evangelicals. In a June 14, 2003 article about a meeting of evangelicals on Muslim-Christian relations in Washington, DC, *World* publisher/CEO Joel Belz discussed the question of whether most evangelicals agreed with Franklin Graham when he called Islam "an evil and wicked religion." Belz argued, "a genuine Christian must believe" that statement was true. He went on to argue that there appears to be a double standard placed upon Christians, effectively driving them from public discourse

"Especially when Muslims regularly use words like apostate and infidel about Christians, I am dismayed that our favorite posture these days is to bend over backwards never to give any offense," Belz wrote, "a pluralism that excludes certain subjects from the debate just because somebody's vocabulary went a little too far in a couple of instances – well, that's no pluralism at all."[434]

The month before, Belz complained: "Why do Muslims get to play by one set of rules, and Christians by another? By what possible measuring stick do we welcome Muslims to this country, even exempting them from taxes when they build a mosque here and otherwise carry on their evangelistic activities – but then agree to tuck

---

[432] Veith, "Lethal 'Gospel," *World Magazine*, 22 February 2003.

[433] "High-Tech Neanderthals," *World Magazine*, 9 August 2003.

[434] Belz, "A Debating Society," *World Magazine*, 14 June 2003.

our tails when someone accuses us of proselytizing a Muslim? After all, it's the Quran that suggests declaring jihad on a nonbeliever who doesn't prove responsive to adoption of Islam ... nothing in Jesus' teaching suggests anything so harsh."[435]

The call for a Christian seat at the table, despite "undiplomatic" comments by certain evangelical leaders, casts an interesting light on a May 22 cover story by *World* National Editor Bob Jones (son of Bob Jones III, president of Bob Jones University). He wrote that the Council for American – Islamic Relations (CAIR) paints evangelicals as hateful, which hurts the cause of constructive dialogue: "Evangelical Christians, who have long been stereotyped as ignorant and backward, can well understand the resentment Muslims feel when they are stereotyped as dangerous and anti-American. But instead of appealing to a shared experience that might bridge a cultural gap between Christians and Muslims, CAIR chose to drive home a verbal wedge between the two groups."[436]

To drive home the message of the double standard between Muslim and Christian discourse in the public square, editor Marvin Olasky conducted a "test of even-handedness" in the mainstream press. He reported that 60 percent of mainstream newspapers "reported as fact" the Muslim account of Abraham's slaughter of a sheep instead of his son Ishmael, over the biblical account of Abraham and Isaac.[437] Olasky also submitted that the grounds for Muslim-Christian relations from an evangelical perspective should be "not to dismiss or avoid interfaith dialogue, but to see it not as a Christian surrender but as a real debate in which Christians try to convince others that Christianity is true."[438]

[435] ———. "Free Speech, For Some," *World Magazine, 17 May 2003.*
[436] Bob Jones, "Truth or CAIR," *World Magazine,* 22 March 2003.
[437] Olasky, "Siding With Islam," *World Magazine, 9 March 2003.*
[438] ———. "Pre-emptive Surrender," *World Magazine,* 9 August 2003.

The Evangelical Press in the Wake of Sept. 11, 2001

Through the pages of the three magazines studied above, three distinct patterns emerge as to a response to the challenge of Islam and Muslims after the Sept. 11th attacks. The editors of CT addressed the issue on the social, the theological, and practical points of contact that relevant to evangelicals.

In terms of the social question, the editors of CT acknowledged that Muslims would now be seen as "enemies" to many, if not most, evangelicals.[439] However, the magazine chose articles and authors that urged evangelicals to build positive, respectful relationships – even to the point of advocating prayer partnerships between Muslims and evangelicals.[440]

On the theological front, CT condemned the fiery rhetoric, as well as the portrayal of Islam as an "evil and wicked religion," by some of the most prominent leaders in the movement. While striving to maintain theological orthodoxy, CT delved into a form of ecumenism by tackling theological questions such as the nature of God in Islam, along with Christianity and its relationship to Muslims. While the answers given may not please the most ardent ecumenist, they attempt to build bridges for Muslim – Christian dialogue by allowing that Muslims have an incomplete (as opposed to a "wicked and evil") understanding of God.[441]

The practical questions after the Sept. 11th attacks center around what position evangelicals should take in the effort by the United States to prevent another Muslim terrorist attack. CT authors approved of military action by the government against terrorists and the regimes that back them. However, it portrayed the option of violence as something that is inherently sinful, but perhaps unavoidable to prevent

---

[439] "Verbal Attacks on Islam Sabotage Evangelism."

[440] Lewis, "Does God Hear Muslims' Prayers?"

[441] Mouw, "The Uncommon Benefit of Common Grace." George, "Is the God of Muhammad the Father of Jesus?"

further death and destruction.[442] In effect, the editors of CT portrayed the seeds of positive, respectful relationships between Muslims and Christians as having fertile soil in which to grow within the realm of evangelicalism.

The editors of the two other magazines also addressed some of the same questions, and sometimes offered widely different conclusions. The editors of *Sojourners* concentrated the majority of their attention on advocating nonviolence. They also condemned remarks by evangelical leaders that Muslims found hateful and divisive. However, Sojo editors did not extend their interpretation of an evangelical social response to active engagement with Muslims beyond political advocacy.[443] *Sojourners* also published one piece on the "power of memory" and the need for themes of peace and reconciliation, but they failed to go beyond the theoretical ideas as to what that would mean for Christians and Muslims.[444]

In this publication, the soil held some nutrients for Muslim – Christian dialogue, particularly in the area of Middle East advocacy for Palestinians. However there were some missing ingredients. *Sojourners* avoided the theological implications of Muslim-Christian encounters, calling only for a unified stance among other religious leaders against war.[445] In the development of their discourse, they severed identification with certain evangelical leaders by condemning Jerry Falwell, et.al. as "fundamentalists" bent on establishing a theocracy.[446]

On a practical level, *Sojourners* grudgingly accepted the need for violence soon after the Sept. 11th attacks, with executive editor David Batstone writing, "justice demands [the terrorists'] punishment."[447] In

---

[442] Carnes, "To Embrace the Enemy."

[443] "Deny Them Their Victory."

[444] James W. Aageson, "Remember This."

[445] "Deny Them Their Victory"

[446] Wallis, "Fundamentalism and the Modern World,"

[447] David Batstone, "A Platform For a Movement," *Sojourners Magazine*, November-December 2001, 15.

susbsequent issues, however, *Sojourners* opposed both the war in Afghanistan and Iraq, and praised the activism of Christian Peacemaker Teams.[448]

On the other hand, the editors of *World* called for better relations with Muslims in some instances, but the overall envirment in the pages of the magazine were hostile to Muslim – Christian relations. *World* defended fiery rhetoric of some evangelical leaders, while condemning similar speech by Muslims as driving a "verbal wedge" between Christians and Muslims.[449] The magazine addressed theological differences by portraying Islam as an "evil and wicked religion" that promotes violence and totalitarianism, while Christianity was portrayed as a religion of democracy and freedom.[450]

World did not grapple with the implications of what CT editors deemed "necessary violence" and Christian teaching on the issue of military force. Rather, it attacked those opposed to war in Iraq and Afghanistan as being on the wrong side of the culture war. In the words of Gene Edward Veith, "The current war on terrorism may be the only conflict in American history in which it is considered insensitive and politically incorrect to criticize the ideology of our enemies."[451]

Religious and social movements define their positions and seek courses of action by what sociologist call a "dialectic between frames and events."[452] That is, the way they define their worldview and their place in society colors how these movements react to events that effect their members. The study of these periodicals show that different segments of the evangelical movement drew upon a variety of principles in response to the Sept. 11th attacks. Sociologists like Robert

[448] Wallis, "Hard Questions for Peacemakers."
[449] Jones, "Truth or CAIR."
[450] Olasky, "Brutality and Dictatorship: How Islam Affects Society."
[451] Gene Edward Veith, "Culture Year-in-Review."
[452] Robert D. Benford, David A. Snow, "Framing Processes and Social Movements: An Overview and Assessment," 625.

Benford and David Snow argue: "movement framing processes are frequently contested and negotiated processes, not always under the tight control of movement elites."[453] That is, the debate among rank and file members of the evangelical movement, not just its most prominent leaders, play an important role in how evangelicals respond to the new challenges emerging after Sept. 11, 2001.

This observation is evident in the fact that the certain "elites" of the evangelical movement, including Franklin Graham and Jerry Falwell, suffered harsh criticism from other segments of the evangelical establishment. Their comments failed to resonate with many looking for a constructive evangelical outlook toward Islam and Muslims. This is not to say figures such as Franklin Graham lost their credibility, as Graham in particular enjoyed a great deal of positive evangelical press coverage long after the Sept. 11th attacks.[454]

In the process of "frame alignment" and social movements, Benford and Snow describe how movement theorists have observed activists engaging in "adversarial framing" to delineate the boundaries between 'good' and 'evil' and construct movement protagonists and antagonists."[455] Nowhere in the press coverage of the challenge of Islam and Muslims after Sept. 11' 2001 is this tendency more evident than in *World* magazine. Given *World*'s relatively high circulation rate (about equal to *Christianity Today*), the worldview of the magazine's editors apparently has achieved a degree of resonance within the evangelical community. On the other hand, *World* does not enjoy the same level of credibility, or have the same extensive web and periodical publishing empire of *Christianity Today*, which offers a much less adversarial view of Muslims and Islam.

Evangelicalism sprang from the need felt by theologically conservative Christian leaders to re-engage with the mainstream, and

---

[453] Ibid.

[454] David Neff and Timothy Morgan, "Jesus Freak," *Christianity Today*, 18 November 2002, 58.

[455] Benford and Snow, 616.

redefine itself with respect to modernism. Even after the Sept. 11th attacks, large segments of the evangelical community have chosen to stay engaged even as the challenges have gone from modern to postmodern. However, the tendencies to retreat and attack from the challenge of the Other has not disappeared from the evangelical movement altogether. Instead, the movement is wrestling with the diversity within itself to negotiate an approach that assures its own existence and its place in the public square. However, the negotiating process has created a family squabble in some instances among segments of the evangelical community, threatening the cohesiveness of the movement in some quarters.[456] The seeds of Muslim – Christian relations fell on uneven ground after Sept. 11, 2001, finding some areas hostile, and some amenable to growth of a particularly evangelical form of ecumenism.

---

[456] Kimball, "Osama and Me."

CONCLUSION

By examining the pages of evangelical magazines and the responses of the movement's denominations and institutions, we can see how Islam and its adherents were transformed in the minds of some members of the evangelical family into a global threat on the scale that liberalism and secularism once held alone. However, the pages of *Christianity Today*, the faculty of Fuller theological Seminary and individuals such as Jamie Winship offered a competing frame in which Muslims were seen, not as a threat, but neighbors with whom they could develop positive relationships (and perhaps a few converts).

The debate among evangelicals over the proper Christian response to Islam and Muslims after the Sept. 11 attacks speaks to the nature of the "family farm" where evangelical ideology is cultivated by its diverse members. The events of September 11, 2001 not only shook the overall American sense of security and isolation from terrorism, it also revealed new fault lines in the evangelical religious landscape.

From theological disputes to social and political responses to Islam, evangelicals once unified by a common character and mission found themselves divided by fundamental differences as to what defines proper engagement and response in the postmodern world. The seeds of constructive discourse and positive dialogue found root in some segments of the new evangelical terrain, and were choked out in others. Some adopted narratives in which Christians should distance themselves from the Other, reflecting fundamentalist tendencies that predate the modern evangelical movement.

The rifts within evangelicalism did not always follow traditional denominational boundaries. For example, while the Southern Baptist Convention and the editors of *World Magazine* cultivated a unified response, the Lutheran Church-Missouri Synod struggled within itself to define it role in interfaith relations. Also, within *Christianity Today* some authors proclaimed "We saw the enemy, and they were Muslim," while others in the magazine encouraged evangelicals to seek out Muslim prayer partners.

Divisions within the evangelical movement are nothing new. Since the earliest days of modern evangelicalism, the Pentecostal/Charismatic portion of the movement remained at odds theologically with non-Pentecostal denominations, and cultural differences grew out of regional and denominational affiliations. Yet, all agreed upon a general common purpose and an essential set of beliefs. That umbrella of beliefs remained largely unchanged before Sept. 11, 2001. However, the new challenges exemplified by Muslims and the religion of Islam have begun to reshape the movement itself.

Bibliography

"2,000 Die in Muslim-Christian Conflict," *Christianity Today,* 7 February 2000, 32.

Aageson, James W. "Remember This," *Sojourners Magazine,* March-April 2001, 40.

Aaron, Sean. "CBN Inaugurates Satellite Broadcasts," *Christianity Today,* 6 October 1997, 89.

Ahlstrom, Sydney E. *A Religious History of the American People.* New Haven: Yale University Press, 1972.

Ali, Maulana Muhammad trans., *The Holy Quran.* Dublin, Ohio: Ahmadiyya Anjuman Isha'at Islam, Lahore, 2002.

Alkhateeb, Sharifa, President, North American Council of Muslim Women. Interview by author, 13 February 2002, Great Falls, VA. Videotape recording. Associated Press, Washington, DC.

Armstrong, Karen. *The Battle for God: A History of Fundamentalism.* New York: Ballantine, 2000.

Athar, Shahid. *Reflections of an American Muslim.* Chicago: Kazi Publications, 1994.

Baker, Barbara G. "Two Filipino Christians Beheaded," *Christianity Today,* 1 September 1997, 86.

―――. "Arab Press Says Hussein Has Returned to Islam," *Christianity Today,* 7 April 1997, 56.

Batstone, David. "A Platform For a Movement," *Sojourners Magazine,* November-December 2001, 15.

Beiler, Ryan. "Spectacular Works, Simple Obedience," *Sojourners Magazine,* September-October, 36.

Begos, Kevin. "Other Baghdad battles Ahead for Christians," *Christianity Today,* September 2003, 29.

Belz, Joel. "Pray For Nominalism," *World Magazine*, 10 May 2003.

———. "A Debating Society," *World Magazine*, 14 June 2003.

———. "Free Speech, For Some," *World Magazine, 17 May 2003.*

Belz, Mindy. "How Much Longer?" *World Magazine*, 13 Dec 1997.

———. "A Christian Opportunity?" *World Magazine,* 11 September 1999.

Benford, Robert D. and David A. Snow, "Framing Processes and Social Movements: An Overview and

Assessment," *Annual Review of Sociology,* 2000.

Berger, Rose Marie. "Calm Before the Storm?" *Sojourners Magazine,* September-October 1996, 14.

———. "A Laboratory of Reconciliation," *Sojourners Magazine,* November-December 1999, 24.

———. "United We Stand," *Sojourners Magazine,* January-February 2002, 34.

Beverley, James A. "Is Islam a Religion of Peace?" *Christianity Today,* 7 January 2002, 32.

"Briefs: North America," *Christianity Today*, July 2001.

"Briefs: The World," *Christianity Today,* 12 June 2000, 27.

Broadway, Bill. "The Limits of Religious Unity," *Washington Post*, 21 November 2001, B09.

Cagney, Mary "Evangelicals Warned Against Persecution Apathy," *Christianity Today,* 18 May 1998, 20.

Calver, Clive. "We've Got To Give Them Back Their Hope," *Sojourners Magazine,* July August 1999, 29.

Carnes, Tony. "In the Belly of the Beast," *Christianity Today*, 12 September 2001.

————. "To Embrace the Enemy," *Christianity Today*, 21 September 2001.

Casey, Ethan. "Pakistan's Despised Christians," *Christianity Today,* 26 April 1999, 94.

Cejka, Mary Ann. "A Miracle in Mindanao, *Sojourners Magazine,* July-August 2002, 42-44.

Chambers, Steve "Can Christianity and Islam Coexist and Prosper?" *Christianity Today,* 25 October 1999, 22.

"Christians and Muslims Still Fighting, Dying in Ambon," *Christianity Today,* 13 November 2000.

"Church Burnings: Muslim Mobs Kill Five in Indonesia," *Christianity Today*, 11 November 1996, 96.

"Churches Challenge Islamic Law," *Christianity Today*, 4 September 2000.

Clarke Peter B., and Ian Linden. *Islam in Modern Nigeria.* Munchen: Grunewald-Kaiser, 1984.

Colson, Charles. "Tortured for Christ," *Christianity Today*, March 1996.

"Conflict in the Holy land," 8 January 2001, 68.

Conflict Transformation Grant: Creating Collaboration and Reducing Conflict in Muslim-Christian Relationships, Fuller Theological Seminary, Spring 2003.

Cooperman, Alan. "Minister's Suspension Over 9-11 Service Lifted," *Washington Post*, 13 May 2003, A07.

Council on American-Islamic Relations. "Florida Mosque Attack Result of Anti-Muslim Rhetoric," News Release. Washington, DC. March 26, 2002.

Dart, John. "U.S. Funds Evangelical – Muslim Project," Christian Century. 27 December 2003.

Davis, James O. "A Biblical Response to America's Emergency," letter, October 2001.

Dayton, Donald W., and Robert K. Johnston, ed. "Some Doubts About the Usefulness of the Category 'Evangelical," *The Variety of American Evangelicalism*. Knoxville: University of Tennessee, 1991.

Dennis, Marie. "Tunnel Vision: How Netanyahu Undercuts the Peace Process," *Sojourners Magazine*, November-December 1996, 11-12.

"Deny Them Their Victory," *Sojourners Magazine*, November-December 2001, 26.

Dixon, Tomas. "Reconciliation Walk: Apology Crusaders to Enter Israel," *Christianity Today*, 5 April 1999, 23.

———. "An Apology, 900 Years in the Making," *Christianity Today*, 6 September 1999, 2.

"Dutch TV Company Broadcasts Threatening Koran Texts by Mistake," *Ananova*.

Efta, Damian. "Who are the Unreached?" *Evangelical Missions Quarterly*, 30, 1.

Emerson, Michael O. and Christian Smith, *Divided by Faith: Evangelical Religion and the Problem of Race in America*, New York: Oxford, 2000.

"Evangelical Christians Strike Breakthrough Accord With Moroccan Government," press release, National Association of Evangelicals, 8 April 2004.

"Evangelical Leaders Urge President Bush to Take Decisive Action to Prevent Slaughter in Darfur," press release, National Association of Evangelicals, 2 August 2004.

"Except for 'The Chopping Off of Hands,' Bremer is Fine With Shariah," *World Magazine*, 22 November 2003.

Fainaru, Steve and Amy Goldstein. "Judge Rejects Jailing of Material Witnesses," *The Washington Post.* April 30, 2002, Page A01.

Falwell, Jerry. "First Person: The 'Loving Rebuke," Baptist Press, 27 May 2003; available at: http://www.sbcbaptistpress.org/bpcolumn.asp?ID=997

"Fear and Hate," *Christianity Today,* 11 September 2001.

Fernando, Ajith. "Bombs Away: How Western Military Actions Affect the Work of the Church," *Christianty Today,* 14 June 1999, 76.

Fiscal Year 2003 Bureau of Justice Earmarks, Department of Justice, 17 June 2003, 2.

Flinchbaugh, C. Hope. "Stolen Daughter," *Christianity Today*, 21 May 2001, 30.

Flowers, Ronald B. *Religion in Strange Times: The 1960's and 1970's.* Macon: Mercer University, 1984.

Fowler, Robert Booth. *A New Engagement: Evangelical Political Thought, 1966-1976.* Grand Rapids: Eerdmans, 1982.

Fletcher, Elaine Ruth. "Orthodox Leaders Closer to Unity," *Christianity Today,* 7 February 2000, 30.

Francis, Vic. "Virgin in a Condom Provokes Outcry," *Christianity Today,* 15 June 1998, 19.

"Friendship Fest Morocco 2005," National Association of Evangelicals, press release, undated.

Jones, Bob. "Truth or CAIR," *World Magazine*, 22 March 2003.

Galli, Mark. "Now What? A Christian Response to Terrorism," *Christianity Today*, 21 September 2001.

———. "Reimagining Francis," *Christianity Today*, April 2003, 107.

Gardner, Christine J. "Congress Approves Modified Religious Persecution Bill," *Christianity Today*, 16

November 16, 1998, 32.

Geisler, Norman, and Abdul Saleeb. *Answering Islam: The Crescent in Light of the Cross.* Grand Rapids: Baker, 2003.

George, Ivy. "The Persecuted Body," *Sojourners Magazine*, March-April 2002, 42-45.

George, Timothy. "Is the God of Muhammad the Father of Jesus?" *Christianity Today*, 4 February 2002, 28.

Gilbreath, Edward. "How Islam is Winning Black America," *Christianity Today*, 3 April 2000, 52.

———. "Taking it Personally," *Christianity Today*, 14 September 2001.

Gopin, Marc. *Between Eden and Armageddon: The Future of Religions, Violence and Peacemaking.* New

York: Oxford, 2000.

"Graham Meets With Iraqi Leaders," *Christianity Today*, 15 November 1999, 15.

Graham, Tim. "Appetite for Evil," *World Magazine*, 27 October 2001.

Stan Guthrie, "A Blast of Hell," *Christianity Today*, 7 October 2002, 16.

————. "Keeping Their heads Down," *Christianity Today*, 18 November 2002.

————. "Christians Fear Muslim Backlash," *Christianity Today*, 12 November 2001, 30.

————. "Deconstructing Islam," *Christianity Today*, 9 September 2002, 37.

————. "Doors Into Islam," *Christianity Today*, 9 September 2002, 34.

————. "Return to Kabul," *Christianity Today*, 21 January 2003, 52.

Haddad, Yvonne Yazbeck. "The Globalization of Islam: The Return of Muslims to the West," Chapter 14, *The Oxford History of Islam*. 1999.

Haddad, Yvonne Yazbeck and Jane Idleman Smith, eds. *Muslim Communities in North America*. Albany: SUNY Press, 1994.

Haddad, Yvonne Yazbeck and Wadi Z. Haddad, eds. *Christian-Muslim Encounters*. Gainesville: University of Florida, 1995.

Harlan, Mark. "A Middle Way in the Middle East," *Christianity Today*, April 2003, 84.

Hasan, Asma Gull. *American Muslims: The New Generation*. New York: Continuum International, 2000.

Herzog, Dawn and Deann Alford. "No Strings Attached," *Christianity Today*, June 2003, 44.

"High-Tech Neanderthals," *World Magazine*, 9 August 2003.

Hollyday, Joyce. "Fire, Wind and Water," *Sojourners Magazine*, November-December 1997, 28-32.

Hulsman, Kees. "20 Coptic Christians Die as Village Tensions Rise," *Christianity Today*, 7 February 2000, 31.

————. "Religious Freedom Delegation Gets Cold Shoulder," *Christianity Today*, 21 May 2001, 28.

Hunter, Susannah. "On the Front Lines With Christian Peacemaker Teams," *Sojourners Magazine*,

September-October 2001, 22.

"In brief," *Christianity Today*, 15 November 1999, 29.

"Islamic Law Proposal Raises Tensions," *Christianity Today*, 7 December 1998, 22.

Juergensmeyer, Mark. *Terror in the Mind of God: The Global Rise of Religious Violence*. Los Angeles: University of California, 2003.

Kasali, David M. "Cursed By Superficiality," *Christianity Today*, 16 November 1998, 56.

————. "Squeezed Between Warring Majorities," *Christianity Today*, 16 November 1998, 68.

Khaldun, Ibn. *The Muqaddimah*. Translated by Franz Rosenthal. Princeton: Princeton University Press, 1967.

Khalidi, Tarif. *The Muslim Jesus: Sayings and Stories in Islamic Literature*. Cambridge: Harvard University Press, 2001.

"Kidnapped Missionaries Reported Safe," *Christianity Today*, 6 August 2001, 28.

Kimball, Charles. "Is Islam the Enemy?" *Sojourners Magazine*, November-December 1998, 16-21.

————. "Osama and Me," *Sojourners Magazine*, January-February 2003, 17-18.

Knippers, Dianne. "Letter to Franklin Graham," Institute on Religion and Democracy, 19 May 2003.

Kurzman, Charles, ed. *Liberal Islam: A Sourcebook*. New York: Oxford University Press, 1998.

Kuzmic, Peter. "Editorial: Bosnia's Bitter Truths," *Christianity Today*; available from: http:www.ctlibrary.com/709

Lawton, Kim A. "The Suffering Church," *Christianity Today*, 15 July 1996.

Lewis, James. "Does God Hear Muslims' Prayers?" 4 February 2002, 30.

Lowes, Carol. "Mercy in Baghdad," *Christianity Today*, May 2003, 27.

"Lutheran President Re-Elected," *Associated Press*, 12 July 2004.

Marquart, Kurt E. *Anatomy of an Explosion: A Theological Analysis of the Missouri Synod Conflict.* Grand Rapids: Baker, 1978.

Marsden, George. *Reforming Fundamentalism: Fuller Seminary and the New Evangelicalism.* Grand Rapids: Eerdmans, 1987.

Matzat, Don. "The Christian in a Culture of Religious Pluralism," St. Peter's Lutheran Church; available at: http://www.stpeter-brooklyn.org/matzat_pluralism.html

McGrath, Alister E. *The Future of Christianity.* Oxford: Blackwell, 2002.

Miller, Bettye Wells. "Shared Religion Viewed as a Vital Tool for Peace," *The Press-Enterprise*, 18 February 2004.

Miller, David Reid. "Philippines: Muslim Separatists Sign Peace Accord," *Christianity Today*, 28 October 1996, 81.

Miller, Kevin D. "Missions' Wild Olive Branch," *Christianity Today*, 9 December 1996, 41.

Minchakpu, Obed. "Nigeria: Muslims Aim to End Televangelism," *Christianity Today*, 2 March 1998, 78.

———. "Islamic Law Raises Tensions," *Christianity Today*, 10 January 2000, 26.

"Missionaries in Harm's Way," *Christianity Today*, 14 June 1999, 19.

Momen, Moojan. *An Introduction to Shi'i Islam: The History and Doctrines of Twelver Shi'ism*. New Haven: Yale University Press, 1985.

Moore, Art. "Justice Delayed," *Christianity Today*, 12 November 2001, 23.

Morgan, Timothy C. "Hebron's Peacemakers Find No Shalom in Olive Branches," *Christianity Today*, 16 September 1996, 92.

———. "Jerusalem's Living Stones," *Christianity Today*, 20 May 1996, 58.

Mouw, Richard. "The Uncommon Benefit of Common Grace," *Christianity Today*, 8 July 2002, 50.

"Muslim Mobs Destroy Churches," *Christianity Today*, 16 September 1996, 112.

Muslims in the American Public Square: Shifting Political Winds & Fallout from 9/11, Afghanistan, and

Iraq, Project MAPS, Zogby International, October 2004.

Neff, David. "Editor's Bookshelf: Thugs in Jesus' Hometown," December 2003, 34.

———. "Editor's Bookshelf: The Erosion Continues," December 2003, 61.

———. " Our Extended, Persecuted Family," *Christianity Today*, 29 April, 1996, 14.

———. "Going to the Prayer Mat for Jesus," *Christianity Today*, 19 May 1997, 4.

Neff, David. and Timothy Morgan. "Jesus Freak," *Christianity Today*, 18 November 2002, 58.

Neuhaus, Richard John and Michael Cromartie, eds. *Piety and Politics: Evangelicals and Fundamentalists Confront the World*. Washington: Ethics and Public Policy Center, 1987.

"New York City Prayer Service," C-SPAN, 23 September 2001; available at:
rtsp://cspanrm.fplive.net/cspan/gdrive/ter092301_nyprayer.rm

"News Briefs," *Christianity Today*, 15 July 1996, 65.

"News Briefs," *Christianity Today*, 1 September 1997, 95.

"News Briefs," *Christianity Today*, 6 April 1998, 27.

Nickels, Beverly. "Saving Bodies, Rescuing Souls," *Christianity Today*, 24 April 2000, 28.

Nimer, Mohamed. *American Muslims: One Year After 9-11*. Washington: CAIR, 2002.

Noll, Mark. *American Evangelical Christianity*. Malden: Blackwell, 2001.

———. *A History of Christianity in the United States and Canada*. Grand Rapids: Eerdmans, 1992.

"Not a Monolithic Bloc: Many U.S. Evangelicals Seek an 'Even-Handed' Middle East Policy,"

Sojourners Magazine, July-August 2003, 24.

Oden, Thomas C. "Death Watch," *Christianity Today*, 21 January 2003, 44.

———. "Whither Christian Unity? *Christianity Today*, 5 August 2002, 46.

Okite, Odhiambo. "Muslim-Christian Riots Rock Nairobi," *Christianity Today*, 8 January 2001, 33.

Olasky, Marvin. "9/11: If We Call, God Will Answer," *World magazine*, 22 September 2001.

———. "Anti-Christian Bigotry," *World Magazine*, 27 April 2002.

———. "A Cold War for the 21st Century," *World Magazine,* 27 October 2001.

———. "Bias is Back: The Post-9/11 Talibanization of U.S. Religious Conservatives Continues," *World Magazine,* 17 August 2002.

———. "Brutality and Dictatorship: How Islam Affects Society," *World Magazine,* 27 October 2001.

———. "Important Dates in the Development of Islam," *World Magazine,* 27 October 2001.

———. "Lights, Camera, Exploitation," *World Magazine*, 19 October 2002.

———. "Pre-emptive Surrender," *World Magazine*, 9 August 2003.

———. "Siding With Islam," *World Magazine, 9 March 2003.*

———. "Spring Treadmill: Books to Get Our Minds in Shape," *World Magazine,* 23 March 2002.

———. "Squandered Inheritance," *World Magazine,* 11 May 2002.

Olsen, Ted. "Mission Leaders Seek to De-Westernize Gospel," *Christianity Today,* 3 February 1997, 86.

———."How Peaceful is Islam," *Christianity Today*, 21 September 2001.

———. "Weblog: Attack Brings Out the Best and Worst of Public Religion," *Christianity Today*, 19 September 2001; available at http://www.ctlibrary.com/8299.

———. "Weblog: Fuller Seminary to Create Interfaith Code of Ethics," *ChristianityToday.com,* 8 December 2003; available at: http://www.christianitytoday.com/ct/2003/149/12.0.html

———. "Weblog: *World* Publisher Apologizes for 'Clumsy' Editorial," *Christianity Today,* 5

October 2001,
http://www.christianitytoday.com/ct/2001/140/52.0.html.

"Operation Blessing Employees Take Off," *Christianity Today*, 28 April 1997, 85.

"Papers of Lemuel Nelson Bell - Collection 318," Billy Graham Center Archives, Wheaton College, Wheaton, Illinois.

"Persecution Goes Global: Over time, Only the Names Have Changed," *World Magazine* 28 November 1998.

"Persecution: Pakistani Bishop's Death Sparks Riots," *Christianity Today*, 15 June 1998, 18.

"Persecution is a Holy Word," *Christianity Today*, December 2003, 32.

"Persecution is Persecution is Persecution," *Christianity Today*, 9 August 1999, 27.

Plowman, Edward E. "Not a 'Senseless Waste," *World* Magazine, 11 January 2003.

Polter, Julie. "A Place Apart," *Sojourners Magazine*, May-June 1997, 28-32.

"Protecting the Right to Convert," *Christianity Today*, 1 March 1999, 28.

Prues, Daniel. "Letter to Pastor Steve Flo," 3 October 2001.

Prues, Daniel. "The Lutheran Church - Missouri Synod Holiday from History: The 25th Anniversary of the Walkout," *Sermons and Papers*. Gravois Mills: Confessional Lutherans, 7 April 1999.

"Publick Occurances," *World Magazine*, 28 December 1996.

"Publick Occurrences: The Week," *World Magazine*, 24 October 1998.

"Publick Occurrences Both Foreign and Domestick," *World Magazine*, 3 April 1999.

"Publick Occurrences Both Foreign and Domestick," *World Magazine,* 9 October 1999.

Pulford, Cedric. "House of Lords Legalizes Human Embryo Cloning," 5 March 2001, 32.

Pundyk, Grace. "Kuwait's Desert Oasis: A Church With 42 Nationalities," *Christianity Today,* 24 May 1999, 22.

Qutb, Sayyid. *Milestones.* Indianapolis: American Trust Publications, 1990.

Rabey, Steve "Mission-Minded Design Strategy for the Muslim World," *Christianity Today* 5 February 1996.

Rahman, Fazlur. *Islam, 2nd Edition.* Chicago: University of Chicago Press, 1979.

Ratliff, Walter R. "Muslim Women After the Sept. 11th Attacks," Video recording. *Associated Press,* 14 February 2002.

————. "Persecution Bills: Congress May Merge Efforts," *Christianity Today,* 7 September 1998, 27.

————. Interview with Brother Andrew, Hilversum, The Netherlands, July 1994.

Records of the Department of Near Eastern Studies, Johns Hopkins University; available from: http://archives.mse.jhu.edu:8000/inv/rg04-090.txt.

Religion and Politics: Contention and Consensus, Pew Research Center 24 July 2003.

Roberts, Patricia C. "Crowds Exceed Palau's Expectations," *Christianity Today,* 27 April 1998, 22.

"Ruling Voids Charges Against Kieschnick," *LCMSNews - No. 97,* 11 December 2001.

Shank, Duane. "Road Map or Dead End?" *Sojourners Magazine,* July-August 2003, 15.

Schlumpf, Heidi. "No Place to Stand," *Sojourners Magazine,* June 2004, 12-16.

Schulz, Wallace. "Schulz Report," Lutheran Church-Missouri Synod, 11 May 2003.

Sellers, Jeff M. "Heightened Hostilities," 9 December 2002, 58.

———. "No Greater Tragedy," 11 June 2001, 95.

———. "How to Confront a Theocracy," *Christianity Today,* 8 July 2002, 34.

———. "Submitting to Islam – Or Dying," *Christianity Today,* October 2003, 100.

Shehested Ken, and Rabia Terri Harris. *Peace Primer: Quotes from Islamic & Christian Scripture & Tradition.* Muslim Peace Fellowship and Baptist Peace Fellowship, Nyack: 2002.

Shibley, Mark A. *Resurgent Evangelicalism in the United States: Mapping Cultural Change Since 1970.* Columbia: University of South Carolina, 1996.

Simon, Bob. "Zion's Christian Soldiers," *60 Minutes,* video recording. CBS, 8 June 2003.

Singh, Manpreet. "Harassed Kashmir Christians Reach Out to Discreet Muslims," *Christianity Today,* 9 September 2002, 26.

Skillen, James W. "Judgment Calls: Genuine Pluralism," *World Magazine,* 7 October 2000.

Smith, Christian. *American Evangelicalism: Embattled and Thriving.* Chicago: University of Chicago, 1998.

Smith, Jane I. *Islam in America.* New York: Colombia University Press, 1999.

Snow, David A. and E. Burke Rochford, et al. "Frame Alignment Processes, Micromobilization, and Movement Participation," *American Sociological Review* (August 1986), 464-481.

Solomon, "Islam," McLean Bible Church, audio recording, 2 February 1991; available from:
http://www.mcleanbible.org//resources/series.asp?SeriesID=26

Solomon, Lon. "Will the Real Antichrist Please Stand Up?" audio recording, McLean Bible Church, 7 January 2002; available from:
http://www.mcleanbible.org//resources/series.asp?SeriesID=30

Stames, Todd. "Southern Baptist Leaders Affirm Vines in Wake of National Attacks," *Baptist Press*, 19 June 2002; available at:
http://www.bpnews.net/bpnews.asp?ID=13645.

Stassen, Glen H., interview by author, Washington, DC, tape recording, 29 September 2004.

Stassen, Glen. "New Paradigm: Just Peacemaking Theory," *Council of Societies for the Study of Religion Bulletin*, Spring 1997.

Stephen, Anil. "Muslim Leader Appeals to Evangelicals," *Christianity Today*, 11 June 2001, 24.

"Stripping Jesus of His Western Garb," *Christianity Today*, 16 November 1998, 65. *The Southern Baptist Journal of Theology*, Spring 2004

Snow, David A. and E. Burke Rochford, et al., "Frame Alignment Processes, Micromobilization, and Movement Participation," *American Sociological Review*, August 1986.

Stone, Peri. "Persecution Propaganda?" *Christianity Today*, 13 July 1998, 14.

Stricherz, Mark. "Evangelicals Advise on Muslim Dialogue," *Christianity Today*, July 2003.

Suhr, Jim. "Lutherans Divided," *Associated Press*, 2 August 2002.

————. "Pastor Cleared After Praying With 'Pagans," Associated Press, 13 May 2003.

Taylor, Jeff. "Christians in Detention for Prayer," *Christianity Today*, 23 April 2001, 27.

"Tight Presidential Race Influenced by People's Faith," The Barna Group, 7 June 2004).

"The Mother of All Liberties," *Christianity Today*, June 2003, 30.

Thomas, Cal. "The Threat Among Us," *Baltimore Sun*, 21 May 2003, 19A.

Twair, Pat McDonnell. "Who is the Veiled Woman," *Sojourners Magazine*, May-June 2001, 40.

Veenker, Jody. "Churches Coordinate Earthquake Aid," *Christianity Today*, 4 October 1999, 22a.

"Verbal Attacks on Islam Sabotage Evangelism," *Christianity Today*, 9 December 2002, 28.

Veith, Gene Edward. "Culture Year-in-Review," *World Magazine*, 28 December 2002.

————. "Lethal 'Gospel," *World Magazine*, 22 February 2003.

"Violence-Weary Muslims and Christians Talk Peace in Nigeria," *Christianity Today*, 18 November 2002, 34.

Volf, Miroslav. "After the Grave in the Air," *Christianity Today*, 21 September 2001.

Wallis, Jim. "A Better Way to Fight Terrorism," *Sojourners Magazine*, November-December 1998, 9-10.

————. "Against Impossible Odds," *Sojourners Magazine*, September-October 2001, 20-28.

————. "A Light in the Darkness," *Sojourners Magazine*, November-December 2001, 7-9.

————. "Disarm Iraq ... Without War," *Sojourners Magazine*, November-December 2002, 7-8.

————. "Fundamentalism and the Modern World," *Sojourners Magazine*, March-April 2002, 20-26.

————. "Hard Questions for Peacemakers," *Sojourners Magazine*, January February 2002, 29-33.

Thomas, Cal. "Idols for Destruction," *World Magazine*, 17 March 2001.

Ur-Rahim, Muhammad 'Ata and Ahmad Thomson. *Jesus: Prophet of Islam*. London: Ta-Ha Publishers, 1996.

Watanabe, Teresa. "Seminary is Reaching Out to Muslims," *Los Angeles Times*, 6 December 2003, B1.

Weisheit, Eldon. *The Zeal of His House: Five Generations of Lutheran Church - Missouri Synod History, 1847-1972*. St. Louis: Concordia, 1973.

Winfrey, David. "Jerry Falwell Attends SBC, This Time as a Messenger," *Associated Baptist Press*, 11 June 1998.

Winship, Jamie. "Christianity and Islam," audio recording, Reston Bible Church, 28 June 2003.

————. "Faith, Hope, Love, Azam," *Discipleship Journal*, September-October 2003; available from: http://www.navpress.com/Magazines/DJ/

Woodberry, J. Dudley. Interview by author, 30 September 2004, Pasadena, Calif., 30 September 2004.

Woodberry, Robert D. and Christian S. Smith, "Fundamentalism Et Al: Conservative Protestants in America," *Annual Review of Sociology*, 1998.

Wright, Rusty. "Christians Retrace Crusader's Steps," *Christianity Today*, 7 October 1996, 90.

Wuthnow, Robert. *The Struggle for America's Soul: Evangelicals, Liberals and Secularism.* Grand Rapids: Eerdmans, 1989.

Yancey, Philip. "Letter From a Muslim Seeker," *Christianity Today*, 3 December 2001, 80.

———. "Why Do They Hate Us?" *Christianity Today*, 1 April 2002, 80.

Zoba, Wendy Murray. "Brother Andrew's Boldest Mission Yet: 'Smuggling' Jesus Into Muslim Hearts," *Christianity Today*, 5 October 1998, 50.

———. "Engaging Our Muslim Neighbors," *Christianity Today*, 3 April 2000, 40.

Zogby, James. Interview by author, Boston, 26 July 2004. Videocassette.

Zoll, Rachel. "Evangelical Leaders Condemn Anti-Islam Statements," *Associated Press*, 8 May 2003.

INDEX

ABOUT THE AUTHOR

Walter Ratliff is the author of the critically-acclaimed Pilgrims on the Silk Road: A Muslim-Christian Encounter in Khiva, and the producer/director of the Emmy Award-winning documentary Through the Desert Goes Our Journey: The Mennonite Trek to Central Asia. He holds degrees from the University of New Mexico, Wheaton College. and Georgetown University. He is currently a content manager at the Associated Press, and an editor with AP's the national religion beat team.

www.ingramcontent.com/pod-product-compliance
Lightning Source LLC
Chambersburg PA
CBHW060921040426
42445CB00011B/726